Memoirs of a Gay Christian Brother

A 90-Year Journey

Bill Stevens, cfc

OUTRUN PRESS

ISBN: 978-0-9965996-1-0

Library of Congress Control Number: 2024936696

DEDICATION

I am writing this memoir for myself. I look back on my life in amazement. At each point, people showed up to bring me to the next stage. Some appeared only briefly, others entered at critical times, and a few were with me on the whole journey. I could not have done this alone, although I consistently sent the message I could. I wrote these pages from very detailed journals, which I kept at specific periods in my life, and many other pages from the memories of a 90-year-old man. So what I have written is not meant to be recorded history, but a sincere attempt to share what was going on in the deepest part of my being during this journey. This is dedicated to all of you, family and friends, who reached out to me in what may appear to be a small way but touched me profoundly, and for which I am deeply grateful.

Bill Stevens is a member of the Congregation of Christian Brothers, a religious congregation founded by Edmund Rice in Ireland in 1802. Bill joined the Religious Congregation in 1951 at the age of 17 and, after his initial formation, taught in their schools for 24 years. His life then took a turn, and for the next 40 years he was a hospital chaplain, created a non-profit organization to reach out to the AIDS community, became a Reiki and Tai Chi teacher, and was a chaplain for a hospice. But this book is really not about that. These memoirs are about the journey of a gay man from birth to the age of 90. We know there were few role models for a young gay man in the '30s, '40s, and '50s. Also, the many hateful and dismissive remarks in both Church and society did not make such a journey any easier. Bill came upon a quotation from Brené Brown which said, "One day, you will tell your story of how you overcame what you went through, and it will be someone else's survival guide." This motivated him to write his story, and he said it would be worthwhile if it were only to help one other person survive.

Contents

1

My Roots

*One day you will tell your
story of how you overcame
what you went through and
it will be someone else's
survival guide.*
—Brené Brown

I am writing my story. I am the last one standing in my generation. There are no other witnesses. It is my truth. My purpose is not to speak ill of others or to judge their lives or motives, but to share the experiences that deeply affected my life. This is the memoir of a gay Christian Brother as he reaches his 90th year.

I need to begin my story with my maternal grandmother, whom we called Mama. She and her family were to have a substantial impact on our lives. Mama was one of seven children of an Irish immigrant father, Matthew Bergin, who came from Ossory County in Ireland. Their mother died at a very young age. Three of the five girls became nurses, and one went into the convent. One of the boys married and had two children, one of whom became an admiral in the United States

Navy; the other boy served in World War I as a medic and died on the streets of Baltimore as an alcoholic—a casualty of this horrendous engagement. The fifth girl, Mary, was the youngest, and her life choices would have consequences for the whole family.

Mama married a doctor, Edward Murphy, whom she met at the hospital where she worked, and they moved to Newport, RI, where he opened his practice. They had two children: my mother, Alice, and her brother, Vincent. They were to go to a boarding school near Baltimore, MD, where their aunt, a nun, was in residence and could keep an eye on them. They then attended Rogers High School in Newport. My dad was a good friend of Vincent, and through this friendship met my mother. Upon Dad's graduation from Cornell University, his life was put on hold as Mama took my mother to Europe after graduating from high school. They traveled to Europe on three separate occasions over the next few years. There was one trip to Italy, one to France, and then a trip encompassing three countries—England, Spain, and Sweden. Our mother frequently told us stories of these trips as we grew up.

Now, how did that happen? At age 20, Mama's youngest sister Mary (1872–1942) became a companion to Charles McTavish (1857–1948), a descendant of Charles Carroll of Carrollton, a signer of the Declaration of Independence. Charles was slightly eccentric, had some erratic behavior, and needed supervision. He lived with his unmarried sister Virginia (1859–1919), and as descendants of Charles Carroll, they had money. They traveled extensively in Europe, and Mary, of course, would go with them. Before Virginia died in

Rome at the age of 60, she asked Mary to marry Charles after she passed and care for him. And Mary did. Mary and Charles continued living in different parts of Europe until 1933, when they returned to the States. They lived in Baltimore, MD and had a summer home in Newport, which they named the Ossory House.

In 1927, my father, Ed Stevens, proposed to my mother. There were issues. My father was not only of English and Scottish descent but also a New England Protestant, and as a result, the rules of the Roman Catholic Church forbade them from having a church wedding. My mother's brother Vincent had eloped earlier with a non-Catholic girl. So Mama was not a happy camper—no church wedding for either child. This would not fit the image she wished to portray to Newport society. My father also had to promise not to interfere in raising any offspring Catholics, which would affect the impact he could have on our lives. They married on November 10, 1927, out of the home of my mother's parents, and moved to a cold water flat in Brookline, MA, close to each of their brothers (Vincent and Bill). My father's brother Bill would become a physician and have three children.

The Stevens side of the family was also not thrilled with my father's marrying a Catholic girl, which resulted in his being disinherited. His father, who owned a Newport bank, died in 1933 of a very painful stomach cancer at the height of the Depression, which was also the year I was born. His mother died in 1935, two months before my youngest sister, Agnes, was born.

My brother Edward was born in 1928, my oldest sister, Mary Ann, in 1930, and my sister Alice in 1932. My brother, as the oldest, remembered how our lives changed dramatically during the Depression years. I once asked him to write down some of his memories for me:

> They were a happily married couple. Dad had an excellent job at a bank and had five children. Then the stock market crashed. After Pa lost his job, I remember him going door to door to sell Ma's jewelry so that he could pay the electric bill.
>
> We sat in darkness when the sun went down. We had boiled potatoes and molasses dinners. I remember Ma bursting into tears when I asked her for a dime to bring to the Catholic school so the nuns could buy supplies for us. She opened her purse to extricate a few coins and flung the dime at me.

The bottom line was that our father did not have money for food, rent, and the necessities of life at the height of the Depression. After my sister Agnes was born, an excruciating decision was made that would drastically change our lives. As noted earlier, Dad's mother, Ada Borden, had died right before Agnes was born. A temporary solution to our circumstances was to move into his mother's home in Newport, RI. Shortly after we moved, I had a severe case of pleurisy, which developed into pneumonia, and I was close to death. I was two at the time. My mother's father, Dr. Edward Murphy, saved my life by placing a drain in my side, not a standard procedure at the time, and I have scars to prove it. It is so interesting that the coincidence of having to move to Newport saved my life.

Mama pressured my mother to move into her home with the five of us while my dad went to live with his brother in Boston to retool himself, going back to school to become an accountant. My brother recalled those days:

> I heard Mama and Mother yelling for four hours straight while I was sitting at the top of the stairs listening to them that whole evening. Mama cursed Dad with every name in the book, calling him repeatedly a bum and other contemptuous terms. She hated him. Ultimately, Mother surrendered, and we moved into Mama's house. Dad would occasionally visit us. I walked in on them once while they were having sex on one of these visits. Dad was unhappy about that; privacy was a huge issue for them. They were still married but separated out of necessity.

There was a time many years later when I got up the courage to ask my father about this part of our life. He was not happy that I did so. The conversation went something like this:

> "What happened that necessitated our move to Newport with Mama?"
>
> "I would like to have done more for you, Bill. I had no other choice. You were taken care of, weren't you? You can't take risks with a wife and five children."

After my dad died, I had the opportunity to write to one of my cousins who was living with my dad while we were living in Newport. I asked her what it was like for her to have had my dad living with them during this time. She wrote:

> Uncle Ed would always pour cold water from his water glass into his coffee to cool it down—to my mother's dismay. He would tell us kids' jokes. "I can wiggle my ears," he'd say, "but I have to have my hat on. See?"
>
> I was a profoundly lonely child in a household that did not have much overt affection and was quite strongly sensitive to how things "should" be. To this day, I remember Uncle Ed gratefully for his kindness to a lonely child. He would come back after a day's studying, taking the train out from downtown Boston on what is now the Green Line, and on it, he would make up puzzles and questions for me. When he got back to the house, we would do them together.
>
> The other day, I was in a group, and we were in pairs talking to the other person about how we felt and what we wanted to say as if they were the significant person in our past life. So I thanked Uncle Ed for his thoughtful affection and love for me and ended up nearly in tears. At the time, it was something I took for granted. But what a difference it made in my life. Uncle Ed was always laid back, and he smiled a lot. That made him different from my parents, too. Looking back on it now, he must have exercised remarkable tact not to disrupt a household and must have missed the

> warmth of his wife and children. So it was good
> for him to make up games for me, too.

I was very grateful that Catherine shared that with me. It brought tears to my eyes too. That could have been us receiving that attention and love. But it wasn't, which is how it was during those years.

A movie called *Cinderella Man* came out. It depicted the life of James Braddock, the heavyweight boxer who won the championship for the first time on June 13, 1935, the day my sister Agnes was born. I often wonder what my dad was doing on that day—awaiting the birth, with one ear glued to the radio?

This movie depicted the deep suffering of the Depression, of which I knew little. We were physically taken care of, but painful decisions had to be made. My dad protected us from many of the miseries and hardships of those times by allowing us to live with our grandmother and receive shelter and food. He trusted that he would bring us all back together again. In the movie, Jim Braddock tells his kids, "We will never send you away." But Braddock had to send them to their grandparents for a while. The heart-wrenching moment in the movie was when they took that step. I can only guess how that was for my mother and dad. It would be seven years before we were reunited.

I will not detail all the events from age 2 to 13 when I entered high school. But during those twelve years, we moved residences twelve times. After seven years with Mama, we reunited as a family in Manchester, CT, and then moved to Binghamton, NY. Things were equally unsettling during WWII, and housing remained an issue. My brother shared with me one of his experiences:

> In Binghamton, NY, I remember the police banging on our front door at 7 am, evicting us for the non-payment of rent. Pa found two rooms downtown at the cheap, low-life Windermere Hotel, into which we were herded. Hookers were cursing and screaming, running up and down corridors. Ma pushing furniture against the room's front door to barricade us from the unknown terrors outside.

Despite these kinds of incidents, Mother and Dad did everything possible to normalize our lives wherever we were. Church and Catholic Schools played a considerable role in this normalization process.

I will end this chapter with a story I only heard much later in life. My family always called me "Bergin." I never questioned that, which says a lot about me. "Bergin" was Mama's maiden name. My brother shared this story with me.

> You were christened William after Dad's brother, Bill. Mama declared, "You should not be called William because then people would call you 'Bill'—a very vulgar and 'common' nickname." Dad, however, never called you Bergin but always called you Bill. He deeply resented Mama's dissing him and his family in this way. I think Mama had pretensions of grandeur as if she belonged to the high-class denizens of Newport "cottages." And Dad and the Stevens family were, as Hillary

Clinton would have said, "deplorables." Taking
his wife and children to Newport was icing on the
cake for Mama. She could do it because she had
money, and he didn't.

That was true. My dad was the only one in the family
that called me "Bill."

2

Seeds Were Planted

My mind was colonized by
the Church.

—Jan Phillips

It is scary to put your story out there, just as it was. I learned what not to do when I was young. I observed the consequences of my older sisters speaking their minds. I learned it was better to keep quiet and reveal nothing about yourself.

My sister Mary Ann once told me the happiest days of her growing-up years were in Brookline, even when the times became difficult. Things changed when we moved to Newport. I was two and had very little memories of those days. But my siblings told me Mama washed our mouths with soap for inappropriate words. My sisters recalled being lined up in front of Mama and being told how ugly they were—for fear they would know they were beautiful. I remember an incident in Binghamton, NY when I was about nine. Mama was visiting us, and she came into the bathroom while I was taking a bath and told me, "Never touch yourself there," pointing to my penis. Seeds were planted. Mama had a consequential influence on our lives.

One of my therapists later in life was an ex-Jesuit, John McNeil. I saw him for five years, and at one point, when he was writing his book *Freedom Glorious Freedom*, with my permission, he used my case history as a separate chapter in his book. He used notes from our sessions and my journals to write the chapter "A Case History of Discernment of Spirits."

From *Freedom Glorious Freedom*:

> I loved my Church while attending grammar school in the Western part of New York State. I attained stability in that area after going through a nomadic period before the five of us enrolled at the parish school run by the Sisters of St. Joseph. I was a familiar face around the Church—a boy soprano in the choir and the ever-faithful, always-available altar boy. My mother made me a complete set of vestments, and neighbors heard me preach the Sunday sermon from my upstairs room.
>
> The charmed relationship with the Church was to change as I entered puberty. I remember an incident after responding to a call in seventh grade to try out for the school basketball team. After the workout, too embarrassed to shower, I looked into the shower area as I left the locker room. I don't remember the exact wording by the coach who confronted me then, but it made a deep and lasting impression. I never returned to another practice session and never participated in any school

sports for the rest of my academic career, although
it was a high-interest area for me. I felt I had done
something very wrong and was a bad person.

I had no one to share this with. I never spoke to my
dad about any personal issues. And I believe that when
he promised to do nothing to interfere with our being
raised Catholic, he thought that he relinquished that
role in our lives. There was no mention of sexuality at
any time in my growing-up years within the family.
Once in high school, when a neighbor was pregnant, my
mother mentioned that a baby was growing in her
stomach and that I should not speak to my younger
sister about it. At no time in my Catholic school years
do I remember sexuality being discussed, except being
told that every sexual thought, desire, or action was
mortally sinful and we would be in danger of hellfire
unless it was confessed and forgiven by a priest. Just
think of that—every sexual thought or desire in itself
was mortally sinful. Also, there was an additional
warning that if you received communion without first
receiving forgiveness, it was a sacrilege. I did not know
precisely what a sacrilege was, but it didn't sound good.
You had to confess that, too. It took me over 50 years to
let all that go. Yes, 50 years—deep seeds were planted.
From *Freedom Glorious Freedom*:

> At the end of my eighth grade, we moved down-
> state New York, and I registered at a high school
> taught by religious brothers. My connection to the
> Church was never the same. It became a place
> where I confessed my sexual thoughts and mas-

turbatory actions to receive forgiveness until the following Saturday. It was a cycle of shame and guilt with momentary peace. In addition, I realized I was attracted to some of the other male students at school. This I never mentioned to anyone. I knew this was wrong and made me a bad person. I had no name to put on it and felt it was unique to me.

My dad had been offered a job in New York City with Remington Rand in 1947 and was able to put a down payment on our first home in New Rochelle, NY. After twenty years of marriage, it had to have been a great feeling for my parents. My oldest brother had just entered the Jesuits before our move, and I was beginning high school. We arrived a couple of months into the school year, and my mother attempted to get me into Blessed Sacrament High School, a parish school. There was no room. Then Brother Vic Chapman, the principal of the school, relented upon meeting my mother, who pleaded my case, and I was enrolled there. It was an all-boys school with all male teachers; in those days, most were brothers. It was a different experience for me. This very male environment was to influence my life.

As early as freshman year, maybe after Vocation Week talks, as I was going to bed one night, I told myself I would be a brother. It came out of the blue—it was just clear to me. And I told no one. As I entered my senior year, I still had not told anyone, including my family. It wasn't until the second half of senior year I shared my desire with Br. Paul McDonald. And he got the ball rolling. I told my mother, who had mixed feelings, because she feared my Dad's reactions. His third child and second son was entering religious life.

My brother had entered the Jesuits. My older sister, Mary Ann, had entered Maryknoll after graduation from St. Gabriel's Academy, and now I was becoming a Christian Brother. Later, my youngest sister, Agnes, would also enter Maryknoll. I am sure it was not easy for my dad to see his second son enter religious life. The only thing I can remember him saying to me was, "Bill, remember to be yourself." Wow. That has stuck with me all my life. I did not realize it would be a lifelong quest.

My mother and I went to New York because I needed to be measured for a black habit. We went to a place on the East Side, and I enjoyed my first subway ride. On this trip, my mother did an extraordinary thing: she bought a ticket to Radio City, and we saw a show together. It was totally unexpected. Another first. It was a touching thing to do for me. That always has been a special memory.

I didn't tell any classmates about joining the brothers, although I think it started to get around. At graduation, I told a couple of friends. I was 17. Shortly after graduation, Br. Patty Reilly, the vocation director, came to our house on Coligni Avenue and took me down to All Hallows Institute in New York City, where a bus was waiting to take candidates to West Park, NY to begin their training. It was a strange journey. I had no idea what I was choosing. But it felt right at the time.

Mother and Dad always supported us in deciding to enter religious life. And the trail to upstate New York was well worn by trips to St. Andrew-on-the-Hudson outside Poughkeepsie, Maryknoll Mother House in Ossining, NY, and now West Park, NY. Everyone would pile into the car with a giant picnic basket with all sorts of goodies, and we would visit on the specified visiting days. Now, I would receive such a visit on the appointed days.

So after moving twelve times, including six cities and six schools, I started my life in the brothers at Santa Maria in West Park with 34 others, where more seeds would be planted.

3

Religious Life

Idleness is the Devil's
workshop.

The sheltered and over-protected life I experienced in my family and twelve years of Catholic schooling helped me smoothly transition to religious life. Preoccupation with sexual thoughts and masturbation ceased during my Novitiate year, only to return with a vengeance during the rest of my formation training.

I hit a roadblock in writing this memoir when I questioned how honest I should be. I reminded myself, this is my story. All those involved in this part of my story are deceased. I will not mention names—those who wish may think they can figure names out—but don't be sure.

My same-sex attraction not only continued but intensified, and my acts of masturbation and sexual desires continued. Filled with guilt, I shared this with one of my superiors in those early years of formation. On one occasion, he had me undress in front of him and gave me some sexual education, which, up to that point in my life, I had never received. On another occasion, I told him about itchiness in my penis, and he arranged for me to see a doctor. The doctor advised that I have a circumcision, and the superior took care of changing my bandages after that procedure. At this time in my life, I was very compliant. I had little knowledge, and I trusted.

At a later meeting, the Superior observed that I kept to myself and did not interact with others. He asked me if there was any particular brother with whom I was comfortable. I told him the name of a brother, and we got to know each other and shared our stories. After a while, I felt pursued by him and tried to find space between us. This only encouraged the pursuit. This intensified and was to be ongoing over the remaining two years of formation. The conflicting emotions over-whelmed me—my fear was paralyzing.

Leaving my formative training and embarking on my teaching mission helped to relieve much of the stress I was experiencing. For the next twenty-four years, I threw myself totally into my identity as a brother and teacher, finding satisfaction in my work. But the deepest core of my being was in constant tur-moil. I was attracted to many of my students, which only heightened my anxiety and fear. The cycle of shame, guilt, and confession continued over the years. I kept my secret. No one else could possibly be experienc-ing any of this. I was uniquely a bad person.

At one point, alcohol helped ease some of the pain. I looked forward to my drink each evening before supper to get me through the night. On the outside, all was well. If you work hard in the brothers, you are readily accepted. I was a workaholic. I had no identity of my own. I had no idea who I was, nor did I know that this would be worth something to find out.

Upon graduation from Iona College, my first teaching assignment was to Victoria, British Columbia, in 1955. I was assigned to teach 63 third graders. To his credit, the Superior hired an elderly, experienced, retired teacher to supervise me in this awesome task. True to his reputation, the Superior had our chores lined up for us on Saturday after five days of teaching and, of course, all sorts of after-school activities. Idleness is the Devil's workshop.

After three years in Victoria, I was assigned to Power Memorial Academy in New York City, where I would spend five years. What a change for me. I remember telling my dad how scared I was as I began my new assignment. It was one of the first honest admissions I ever shared with him. The school was a ten-story building with six floors of classrooms and 15 or more brothers living on the top floors overlooking the New York skyline. Looking back, I realize I did not spend even one day enjoying anything in New York. It never entered my mind. School absorbed my life from the crack of dawn when we had our morning prayer to when I collapsed in bed at night. I laugh when I remember the first few nights when I heard a siren outside my bedroom window. I would run to my window to catch the sights and sounds, but sadly, that did not last long. Sirens become part of your life in the Big Apple.

At one point during my years at Power Memorial, I knew I needed to talk with someone about my unresolved sexual issues. I was to make final vows in June 1959. I asked my brother if he knew of anyone I could see, and he, always there for me, gave me the name of a priest psychiatrist at Fordham. I saw this priest a couple of times, and he then referred me to a psychiatrist on Park Avenue in the City. Really? Park Avenue? I went and had my session. Shortly after, I received a hundred-dollar invoice. I never had asked permission to go, and in no way would I let my Superior know I needed to see a shrink. That would make one a marked man in the '50s. I managed to pull together the money from some rental funds from the gymnasium I oversaw. End of therapy. It would be twenty years before I made another attempt to see a therapist, which also ended dramatically.

A story about the Province Leader in the '60s showed that it was dangerous to be in his line of vision when he was thinking about making assignments for the following year. Not only for the obvious reason, but he also mixed names with faces more than once, and one would end up scratching one's head when getting a new assignment. In the summer of 1963, I received notice while studying in Washington, DC that I was assigned to teach in Dominica in the West Indies. I looked at a map and saw the dot. Who was he sending? Me? Really?

This assignment was to change my life in so many ways. I can't put into words how important it was to be away from everything I had known up to that time. It was like turning over a new page. I was away from my family, the Provincial, and the incessant work at the school. It was a new life. I grew up. I gained confidence and began to get in touch with my gifts.

Thanks be to God, so many kids were hungry for knowledge. They were intelligent and tenacious students. We prepared them for the Cambridge Exams. They were highly motivated because it was their ticket off the island or landing a government job. They made you look good as a teacher. I also became involved in the larger community—becoming treasurer of their national sports association, coaching their national basketball team, and creating the first-ever outdoor Island night basketball league on the school grounds.

Then, the Superior General decided that Canada should take over the West Indies mission and the Americans should work on the missions in South America. That was a painful change for me. I was assigned to teach at Iona Prep in New Rochelle.

But I was a different person when I returned. There was no adjustment period. I was back into the fray. I had missed all the turmoil of the '60s—the assassinations, the riots, and the societal changes. I felt lost.

Three things happened on my return that strongly impacted my life. First, I moved close to my parents, who now lived in an apartment in Larchmont, NY. I was also closer to my sister Mary Ann who had recently divorced and was struggling with four young boys. I felt my mother had huge expectations that I would make all my sister's problems disappear. And I always thought I needed to do more. Second, my only close friend in the brothers, who had joined the brothers with me and with whom I had touched base often and spent time whenever I could, decided to leave the brothers. He could not tell me personally. He asked the provincial leader to do that. The whole episode was painful, as I lost my best friend. Third, I was shocked when, two years later, I was asked to be Superior of a community at Bishop Gibbons High School in Schenectady, NY. It was a large community, diverse in age, and had gone through three superiors over a short period. I accepted the assignment but did not feel up to the task.

I was six years at Bishop Gibbons and experienced three different school principals. Each of them played a crucial role in the evolution of the school from an all-boys Christian Brothers School to a co-educational Diocesan High School when it merged with a nearby Catholic girls' school run by the Sisters of Notre Dame. This would be the first co-educational high school in our Province.

I went into my usual survival mode by throwing myself one hundred percent into the middle of things. I was Superior and Treasurer for the Community, taught classes, coached a basketball team, and eventually became school treasurer and played a role in the merger of the two schools.

Toward the end of my time at Bishop Gibbons, we buried Br. Xavier Dunphy, the senior brother in the Community who had a long illness. Then, there was a five-month period when things began to wind down for me, and I could take a breath. I knew my six years as Superior were coming to a close, and I was not only tired, but I knew I needed to address some deeper issues that my workaholism would not solve. I heard of a psychiatrist nearby that someone recommended and took the risk of seeing him without letting anyone know. I had a minimal number of sessions and was able to begin to open up. One day, as I appeared for my next session, the secretary told me my therapist had died. Yes, he had died—end of therapy.

No break. My next assignment was Essex Catholic High School in the inner city of Newark, NJ. It was a mammoth old insurance building converted into a high school and a residence for over twenty brothers. There are three things I remember most from my one year there. First, my parents celebrated their 50th wedding anniversary in 1977. Second, I met a brother in the Community who would become a supportive friend, Rich Venturi. He was a free spirit who marched to his own drum and paid the price for it. And third, at the end of that year, I got a call and was asked to be the Superior of Catholic Memorial Community in Boston, MA. This blew my mind.

During a retreat in Newark, I spoke with a priest about some of my issues, and he encouraged me to start therapy. I was determined to take care of myself in this way, finally. When I got this call and was asked to be Superior in a community once again, I said I would take the position but was upfront and told the Province Leader that I intended to start therapy for myself while in that position. He said okay, but I don't think he knew what he was saying okay to.

I went to Catholic Memorial High School in the Boston area. It would be my last year of teaching. I started therapy with a priest connected to the House of Affirmation, a therapeutic residence in Rhode Island for religious and priests. I went to see him faithfully and secretly on a very regular basis. He created a very safe space for me. I was with someone who cared about me as a human being and not about what I could do. After a few months of one-to-one therapy, I started attending group therapy sessions and began to realize I was not alone with my fears as I listened to similar stories to mine.

It was another challenging year. It became clear to me that I was dying in the classroom. It was no longer life-giving but was draining me emotionally and physically. Despite hours of preparation, I felt inadequate and alienated from my students. I found the courage to write a letter to the Province Leader and indicated that I could no longer teach but would be willing to stay on as Superior of the Community. However, a new brother was appointed superior when the senior brothers in the Community indicated they could not support a superior who was not teaching in the school. At first, I was hurt by this, but I was able to let go of it.

I had planned a 30-day silent retreat in July long before this occurred. It was to be at the Thomas Merton Contemplative Center in Magog, Ontario. And what an oasis that was for me. For the first time, I did nothing but relax and listen in a beautiful, supportive, loving environment under the guidance of incredible spiritual directors. Other brothers who had been there told me I would be in a safe place and would be in good hands. And they were right. Retreats would become integral to my healing for the next part of my journey.

So, I ended my 24 years of teaching ministry as a religious brother living in a community of brothers. I had no clue where this next step would take me.

4

The Taboo Topic

I was 26 before I knew.

I came across a well-written article by Brother G. T. Faulkner entitled "Congregational Culture: Our More Recent Story." I am incorporating the passage below from this article because it powerfully depicts what was going on for me during formation and how this taboo topic had a powerful influence on my whole life.

Br. Faulkner wrote:

> To the best of my knowledge, no formal research has been published on the positive and negative impact of church and Christian Brother culture on members of our Congregation. What follows, therefore, is speculative rather than scientific thought, provoking rather than definitive. . . .
>
> There is no doubt that official church teachings on sexuality, mainly as mediated through the family environment and the Catholic school, and later on through formation practices in religious congregations, including our own, played a highly significant role in the formation of negative atti-

tudes and practices in many people. Most of the brothers I spoke with regretted the almost total lack of attention to education on sexuality in their families and Christian Brother Schools. The brothers who taught me "seemed very uneasy in talking about sex" was a common statement. The same statement was expressed almost universally in formation programs, except in more recent times.

Catholic morality, especially sexual morality, was basically prohibitionary. The rules were of the "thou shalt not" variety. Against each prohibition was a threat of punishment. In the sexual area, all matter was considered "grave." This was taught so exhaustively that "full knowledge" could hardly be denied by the transgressor. Leaving only the question of "full consent." How was the child to consider the delicate matter of consent? They would all likely be frightened into accepting full responsibility lest they be accused of hiding a "mortal sin." We inherited a very-much-alive tradition of corrupted sexuality, and we were seldom free from fear. One serious consequence was an avoidance of intimacy because intimacy is freedom from fear.

Sex was a taboo subject both in the family and in the wider church. It was as if sexual understanding and growth were put on hold while other areas of life—intellectual, physical, cultural—went ahead regardless. One former province leader told me, "I was 28 before I knew." There

was a culture of strict secrecy about sexual matters.

One result was a fear of sex as something dangerous, even evil, and therefore to be avoided
even in conversation. We were warned about "bad
thoughts," so the apparent escape was to avoid
matters sexual at all costs, to repress, to flee, to
deny, to treat as taboo. All matter was "grave."
Sexual sin was the big sin. The resultant silence
and secrecy led to repression and denial and, over
the years, to a lessening ability to dialogue about
sexuality in any form.

I identify with each of the above words one hundred
percent. This was my experience, even to the statement,
"I was 28 before I knew." I was 26. I debated within
myself for an extended period whether to incorporate
this chapter into my memoirs. But why would I not
include something I struggled with all my life? You take
a vow of chastity at the age of 18, and then that is the
end of the story? That is not the way it was for me.

From the age of puberty, sexuality was a huge issue
for me. How could I have allowed myself to be brain-
washed that every sexual thought, desire, or action was
mortally sinful and brought that into my lived life? It
was an integral part of my journey, and I am ashamed
and embarrassed to put that in writing. But it is part of
my story. I realize it wasn't a unique experience. Many
were exposed to the same things, but I embraced the
entire package more easily and hung onto it longer
because of my history.

When I shared my story, experiences, and thoughts with a good friend of mine, much later in life, who also was a therapist, she wrote to me:

> I cried throughout your email—that my dear friend and incredible person, Bill, has been tortured so much by family, who should have loved him more wisely, by a church that should have fostered healthy sexuality in him, and by a society that conspired to keep his beautiful nature repressed. I cry for my friend . . . my heart can only say . . . you are beautiful as a child of God.
>
> Some other thoughts . . . your attraction to the students when you were a teacher . . . this is because you were not allowed to express your sexuality with peers . . . had you a lover/partner all through your life, you would have found these young fellows attractive . . . but you would not have been in the torment you were in . . . all of us are attracted to the ones that we find interesting and beautiful . . . but when most of us have healthy peer sexual relationships we are able to satisfy those fantasies. . . . I am sad that you would have feared yourself so much and thought yourself as bad and unworthy. . . . Bill, God cried at your suffering . . . it was man/the church that spoke words that were ugly and critical of sexuality and then labeled them "God's words" . . . NO NEVER WOULD A GOD I KNOW DIRECT PEOPLE TO REJECT THIS PART OF THEMSELVES . . . and so . . .
>
> You move away from this ugly institution . . . a thing proclaimed as the love of God but demon-

strates hatred of creation . . . what logic here . . . give me a child until the age of 7, and I will have him the rest of his life!!! THERE IS NO GOD WHO WANTS WHAT THIS CHURCH HAS ESTAB-LISHED . . . trust me in this, and I know shit about God and theology . . . yet . . . I say trust me . . . I know this . . . I know that you are not in moral danger . . . I know this . . . not one day in my life have I wondered, "Am I saved?"—why, I don't even know what that expression really means actually . . . I do know "grace" . . . I do know we are all returned in spirit to the creator. . . .

So, as you wonder what your next steps should be . . . go deep and find that place that still feels threatened and terrorized by the church and vanquish this within you . . . this will help you open up to the sexuality you are so afraid of . . .

I am here for you, Bill . . . much of what you have shared in your email, you had already shared with me throughout the years. . . . I did not understand how the brotherhood experience continued to shame you so deeply . . . to traumatize you so much more. . . . I fully get why your life energy is stalled deep within your spirit . . . and it can be released.

She was one of my very special friends who supported me on my journey.

5

A Breakthrough

*We all have to make deci-
sions in life—some right
and some wrong. But really,
none are wrong because it is
what we feel is right at the
time.*
—*My Dad*

I was now embarking on a journey into the depths of my soul—a place where I never wanted to go and could not go alone. A friend of mine had just completed a Clinical Pastoral Education Program and suggested this possibility to me. Most CPE programs were filled by late August. Upon returning from my silent retreat in Magog, I applied late to the program at St. Raphael Hospital in New Haven, CT. This would begin a series of serendipitous experiences as I started my healing journey into the unknown.

I got a call from the program director and went to New Haven to meet with him, and I was accepted. Acceptance at such a late date was quite unusual. But this was the first of many remarkable things to happen on a journey I often felt I had no control over.

It was a nine-month program, and I lived in a residence next to the hospital. A CPE program helps you connect with areas of your life that are blocks to your ministry to others. It would be my stepping stone to my next thirty years of ministry—ten years in hospital chaplaincy, twelve years of AIDS ministry, and ten years of hospice work.

A significant moment during this CPE program played a huge role in changing my life. It may sound insignificant, but it was transformative. After I completed three months of the program, my supervisor challenged me to wear a suit and tie rather than my black suit and collar while in the hospital. For 30 years, from the age of 17, I had worn my black habit or suit and collar—that was who I was to the world and to myself. I remember going to a department store and buying a colorful jacket, shirt, and tie. When I walked into the hospital the next day, I was very self-conscious before realizing no one cared. They accepted me as I was. I was Bill, who also happens to be a brother, rather than being a brother—making this my identity— allowing another person to define me. When I walked into a hospital room with my black garb, I was immediately identified as a priest, and I was explaining who I was not. I now no longer had anything to hide behind. I never wore my black suit, habit, or collar again for the rest of my life.

After my CPE experience, my congregation permitted me to apply for a position as a hospital chaplain in Syracuse, NY at Crouse-Irving Memorial Hospital. I also lived with the De La Salle Brothers community there because we had no community in Syracuse. I worked for two years with a wonderful team at the hospital. Fr. John Rose was a special guy—young, enthusiastic, open. He supervised me and the religious sisters who, at different times, joined the pastoral program. We all had our reasons for doing so. This was an exciting Vatican II time in the Church, and some religious brothers and sisters were moving out of the classroom into different spheres of ministry.

These two years were my training ground. To go on the floors to visit patients and be called to the emergency room and be with dying patients were part of your daily life—eight hours a day, five days a week. Sometimes the emotions were raw, sometimes misunderstandings occurred with those you worked with, and sometimes, you were just exhausted. You had to learn to take care of yourself, even if it meant taking time out when needed, asking someone to listen, or reaching out to someone who had gone through a tense interaction.

Fr. Jim Carey was a great supervisor of the pastoral care teams operating in the diocese and brought us together periodically at a beautiful retreat center to recharge ourselves. At these events, we got to know each other and learned to laugh at ourselves and experience each other differently.

So it was difficult for me to leave this caring environment and pursue the coordinator of pastoral care position at Community General Hospital when a Holy Cross brother was leaving that position. It was on the other side of town, and I saw it as an opportunity to take more of a leadership position. I was ready for the challenge.

In this position, from August 1982–July 1984, I was not only chaplain at the hospital with Sister Rose, a Sister of St. Joseph, but also was responsible for alerting the priests from the local parishes about the admission of one of their parishioners, especially if the person was to undergo serious surgery or was entering the end stages of life. We developed a system in which any priest doing his normal visit would check in at the front desk, where names of the patients who needed the sacrament of the sick or would like to see a priest would be left. It worked very well and lowered the number of calls received at night for such services, which was appreciated by the clergy.

During my four years in Syracuse, I grew in ways I could never have imagined. However, the province leadership consistently told me during these years that I must seriously consider living in one of our communities or leaving the Congregation. My work would be blessed only if I lived in one of our communities. This was the ultimatum. And I was given a year to decide.

I moved into a tiny apartment that I found a couple of blocks from where I worked. I did this a day after my fiftieth birthday in 1983. For the first time, I was fully responsible for myself. And as this year of discernment began, I explored different options.

My spiritual director suggested priesthood. I went through a discernment process with the Diocese of Syracuse, seeking acceptance as a candidate. The application included a visit with a psychiatrist. He gave a very accurate report. The personality test scores showed that I was sensitive to others, felt sorry for myself, kept my problems from others, and was independent and autonomous. (No surprises here.) Other tests showed that I had repressed sexuality and issues with authority. (No surprises here.) Application declined.

I struggled between being on my own and creating my own life or being drawn back to the community to be secure and safe. Ultimately, I took what is technically called exclaustration. You were on your own but could apply to return within three years. I knew it was the right thing for me to do.

After two years, leaving this ministry at Community General Hospital was difficult. I could have stayed, but I needed to take a complete break to honor the time given to me for the discernment process. Sr. Rose, at first reluctantly, took over my position and was to do an excellent job.

Telling my family was very difficult. On a visit home when I was alone with my parents, I told them what I planned to do. I knew my mother would be very upset, and she did not disappoint. To have had four children join religious life and now to have all of them leave broke her heart. I know she took this as a judgment of herself. I came off the pedestal. I now had no identity and felt rejected for trying to be myself for the first time. I had received all my affirmation by being a Christian Brother and acting the way others expected me to act. But deeper still, I was leaving home for the second time. The brothers had taken care of me since the age of 17.

At the end of my visit, my dad surprised me by saying we all have to make decisions in life—some right and some wrong. But really, none are wrong because it is what we felt was right at the time. He continued by saying I had done good for many people over the years, and he was sure that I would continue to do good and that he would pray for me. My mother expressed disappointment, but although she always had an initial strong, honest, spontaneous reaction, she never wanted to shut you out forever. It was so huge for both my parents to express what they did.

In one of my last meetings with my therapist, Sr. Maureen, as I was discerning my decision to leave, she asked, "Haven't you left the community already?" And I had to look where I was at:

- Living in a city where we have no community
- Choosing to do work that no one else is doing
- Having no contact with any existing community
- Having little contact with the province leadership team
- Living entirely on my own
- Not wearing a black suit, habit, or collar
- Finding no life for me in the communities I visit
- Finding little common ground with the brothers when I do visit

By the end of the year, I let the leadership know that I would take exclaustration from the congregation. I resigned from my position at Community General

Hospital without knowing where I would go or what I would do.

6

The Next Step

*Closed doors indicate that
the right door has not yet
opened.*

I did what I believed in my gut was right for me, but
it did not take away the doubts. I never felt so
scared in my life. The next step was to find a job as a
lay hospital chaplain. I applied to all the job openings in
the *National Catholic Reporter* and flew to Kalamazoo, MI
for an interview. Really? Yes, I was desperate. I realized
I had more qualifications than the Director, and I was
not surprised when I was not accepted for the chaplaincy position there. It gives me goosebumps to think
how my life would have changed if I had gotten the job.
It was hard to trust that closed doors meant the right
door had yet to open. But then it did. There was a job
opening for Vice President of Pastoral Care at St. Peter's
Medical Center in New Brunswick, NJ, as supervisor of
two priests and five nuns in the department. I applied.

When I heard that Sr. Agnes was doing the interview, it brought back memories from 1982 when I heard
of an opening at Calvary Hospital in New York, where
the same Sr. Agnes was interviewing for an open chap-

laincy position there. I responded because of the pressures on me to live in one of our communities. I was on the first leg of my journey to the interview with Sr. Agnes, about twenty miles into the trip, when my unreliable car broke down completely, and I was towed into a closed gas station garage at 5 pm. A gentle snow began to fall as I left my motel room for a sandwich. On my return, I slipped on an embankment, fell, and broke my ankle. I went back to Syracuse by ambulance to the emergency room at the hospital where I worked and limped around in a cast to the knee for the next two months. I had to cancel my interview for the job at Calvary. And we think we are in charge of our lives.

Sr. Marie de Pazzi was a sister of St. Joseph of Peace and was the president of St. Peter's. I heard later that Bishop McCarrick, Chairman of the Board of St. Peter's Medical Center, was not thrilled about having a brother on exclaustration as Vice President of Pastoral Care. But Sr. Marie wanted me there and fought for it. You did not mess with her. I was to be there from August 1984 to February 1989. I learned that Sr. Agnes was tough on the five sisters on the pastoral care staff. They did not get away with much. She was much like their novice mistress, and they resented it—especially in the '80s after their hard-fought battles with their congregations for more freedom.

So, here comes Bill, who has issues dealing with and interacting with women. Did they test him? Immediately. Each one found his vulnerability, which was relatively easy to find. So I was confronted constantly, and I learned from painful experiences.

All the personal issues that were revealed during my therapy and direction in Syracuse did not go away but only became magnified. But I could now read the signals that I needed help moving forward. I could not do this alone. I needed to continue my therapy in New Brunswick. And the universe provided. Joan deVelder, who was to become a lifelong friend, gave me the resources to find Gordon Boals, a psychotherapist.

Gordon Boals summed up my whole life in a nutshell after only a few sessions with me:

> You have always been unable to express your anger. When you saw your mother expressing her anger and not allowing anybody to talk back (a slap, if they did), you decided never to express your anger but to withdraw and be stubborn—keeping everything and all feelings to yourself. This was your punishment to your mother.
>
> You decided to separate yourself from family.
>
> You now have lots of unexpected anger at your mother for never allowing you to express your feelings and at your father for never standing up to your mother and never reaching out to you, leaving you alone in the world you created for yourself.
>
> Whenever you talk to them, and this anger comes up, you shut down. This pattern shows itself with other people as well. You choose not to communicate rather than express your true feelings because they never counted as far as your mother was concerned.

The two things that bring us in contact with
other people are sex and anger. These are your
two greatest fears.

Wow! What a revelation. I saw my family regularly
out of obligation. But long ago, as a child, I had decided
to enter my protective shell and allow nobody in, no
matter what. That was my survival stance. No one
could hurt me there. But I deeply wounded myself.
Gordon Boals also shared this with me:

You need two normal people to have a normal relationship. Do not crucify yourself that you are
unable to have a normal relationship with members of your family.

Your dad modeled a behavior pattern for dealing with your mother. It is not the only way to
deal with it. But withdrawal is one option. She
cannot finish your unspoken thoughts.

Your life was planned by your mother and by
the Congregation. You seldom created something
for yourself. You need this space now to be free
from your mother and the brothers and create the
lifestyle you want. Take time to imagine what you
want, how you want to live, how you want to use
your time.

You do not permit yourself to get on with your
life, to become independent of your mother and
live and enjoy life. There is a strong force within
you that will not allow you to consider what you
want to do.

These profound insights gave me pause. Becoming conscious of these behavior patterns was the first step, but changing my relationship with my parents and other authority figures was challenging.

It just brought home to me what conditional love was all about and how devastating it can be for me when I realize I have not lived up to another person's expectations. So often in my life, up to this time, I was very conscious that I could pay a heavy price to act in my self-interest.

Gordon Boals added:

> You now have the option. Please someone and get false acceptance, or be your own person and risk experiencing genuine pain. But you can survive this pain and go on living and be free.

And, of course, this all applied to the brotherhood as well. I discovered that I did not have to choose between being Bill Stevens and being a brother. Up to this point, being a brother meant playing a role and putting on a mask. We were never taught to be ourselves and discover who we were. Gordon encouraged me to find out that being Bill Stevens and being a Christian Brother could be the same, and I did not have to choose one or the other. So, my discernment continued.

Gordon pointed out my intimacy issues:

> You do not withdraw from people so much, but you try not to let people in. You fear intimacy. You fear demands and manipulations and know your inability to say no to them. It is not that you do not know how to behave or what to say, but

you are afraid to be intimate. You do not share yourself when you want to.

Jim Dolan, my spiritual Director in Syracuse, had told me:

> No one can subjugate you if you are free. No one can dominate you unless you say "yes." No one can take away your freedom. If someone is "dumping on you," don't place yourself by the garbage can and allow it to happen.
>
> It is okay to please others, but it is not okay to please them so they accept you. Because then, you are nice to them but hate them because of their power over you.

What wise people I was gifted with at this point in my life.

7

Parallel Journey

*I am Bill Stevens, who has
eros.*

Bill is truly human.

*Open the doors of your
heart.*

*Allow eros —pleasure —
delight into your life.*

At this time of my life, I was in need of religious imagery to heal me—the very imagery used to colonize my mind. I otherwise could not let go of the imagery that killed my spirit.

A year after my CPE experience in New Haven, I experienced the death of a very close friend named Peter. I knew Peter as a brother while I was teaching in Boston and knew he was having a difficult time in the classroom. He was very charismatic and had many beautiful spiritual gifts that could have been used in different ways. But it was not to be. Peter left the Brotherhood, and within a year, he was tragically hit by a car while waiting for assistance after running out of gas on a major highway. My spirit was crushed.

I knew I needed to go on an eight-day retreat. Br. Jack told me about Gloucester, a Jesuit retreat house in Massachusetts situated at the tip of the state and over-looking the Atlantic Ocean. I went there in June, 1981. When I looked back on my notes in my journal, I was shocked when I saw what I had written after the first session with my director:

> I was able to tell my director that I was uncom-fortable with him, that he talked too much and did not know where I was at in my journey, and that I had felt disconnected from him when I filled up with emotion while sharing the death of my friend, Peter.

I can't remember saying those words, as it was unlike me to do so, but it helps me recall the intensity with which I entered the retreat and my determination to make the best of it.

I read a book entitled *Healing Memories* on the retreat and was drawn to this passage:

> Don't lie to God. We lie to God by saying what we think we should feel rather than what lies within our hearts. Feelings are always present but not always heard; write out feelings when you begin prayer or speak feelings out loud to Christ—that helps catch what sounds sincere and what is phony.

After reading this, I decided to walk on the beach, and as I left the room, I asked Jesus to walk with me. I wondered why I had such difficulty giving and receiving love. I asked him if a past hurt needed to be healed. The response was immediate. *What about X?* But that was 30 years ago! Yet I knew it was true. I returned to the house to get a sweater and a handkerchief. I was using delaying tactics but knew I had struck gold.

Once on the beach again, He hit me with *what about Y?* Wow! I could not believe it. I sat on the rock at the far end of the beach and was able to experience all the hurt and the pain once again. This had never come up during my CPE experience. This was a reason for my sense of isolation and withdrawal from intimacy. And I cried and cried. (X and Y were about my formation experiences)

As I sobbed, I felt His presence; I felt His love for me. I felt His care. He had been with me these 30 years and was with me now to heal the pain. I was there for over an hour and a half. I just went deeper and deeper. When it was time to see the director, I got in the room and cried openly for another 30 minutes for the pain and His love. My director and I were now connected.

In July 1983, I attended a workshop at Christ the King Retreat House in Syracuse, a few blocks from where I lived. And incredibly, I fell in love with a sister during the time I was there. How did this happen? It just did. It was just a random encounter. I wrote in my journal:

I fell in love with Sister J—I can't believe it. It is 3 a.m., and I have only gotten two hours of sleep. I know His hand is in this. I never thought it would ever happen to me. I am confused, happy, and scared, and I have a life surging through me that I have never experienced before. I don't want to do anything to harm it.

I don't know if she cares for me in the same way. I hope to ask her that today. I don't know where this will lead, but I know it will change my life in good ways if I can keep my head, not run away, and control my fears.

I know this will make me vulnerable and can be so painful. But this time, I want to take this risk. He waited until I was ready. Am I prepared to handle this? Fear is all that is in the way.

I smile as I look back on this. I couldn't say goodbye at the end of the workshop as I felt she was showing affection to another participant, which broke my heart. I had uncontrollable tears running down my face all during the closing Mass. I could not believe these emotions were happening. I had never experienced these feelings before. I realized how immature I was in the area of relationships.

I made many attempts at writing a letter and saw this in my journal (which I wrote but never sent):

7/12/83

Dear J,
I fell in love with you during the workshop. I think you are a beautiful and compassionate woman. I re-

gret that the 18-year-old part of me could not express this to you at the time, and I especially regret that I could not say goodbye to you on Thursday.

I hope I did not cause you any pain. I appreciate your acceptance of my efforts to communicate what I could.

Instead of following my usual pattern of running away from all of this, I am taking a risk by sharing it with you. If you want to continue this relationship, I would be open to it.

I want to leave you free to respond however you wish. The fact that we spent some time together and I have been able to write this to you has been a new growth for me in this relationship area.

Whatever your response, I hope I will be older the next time we meet—I am 20 now. I will be working on it.

Of course, all of this was brought up in therapy. It became evident that once I was aware of my sexual feelings, everything became bad—I was bad, the relationship became bad, and my feelings were sinful. So it wasn't surprising that I ran away from her the next day and couldn't tell her everything I wanted. I could not sit by her and naturally talk to her because I was bad.

When I got home after therapy, and before I sent the planned letter, I received a letter from her asking to pursue the relationship. I wrote in my journal: "It gave me feelings that I never experienced before. I feel loved and cared for by another person for the first time."

We met once or twice after. We were able to terminate the relationship in a better way. It was at this period of my life that I was dealing with exclaustration issues and possible priesthood. It was just something that happened when I was in a very vulnerable period and feeling very much alone, confused, and unsure of my future. But at the same time, it was a beautiful gift, although I in no way knew how to deal with it—at age 50.

Three years later, in July 1986, I went to a retreat in Bangor, PA, in Kirkridge. I can't remember the exact title of the retreat (Eros) or the presenter (Bishop Spong?). I was still on exclaustration and doing my best to explore this area of my life. This retreat was to be a very profound experience for me. We broke into small groups and stayed in the same groups for three days. Some notes from my journal:

> *God has sent me a beautiful gift to help me work through my sexual development.*
> *What beautiful people.*
> *So much pain and hurt.*
> *So much love and healing.*
> *So nonjudgmental.*
> *I think God is calling me to more love in my life and will fulfill my desire for a companion on my journey.*
>
> *Diane:*
> *so willing to help me be healed*
> *offer of self completely*
> *offer of her love*
> *immense compassion and understanding and*

> *gentle*
> *ability to be with*
> *totally present*
> *so vulnerable*

At the end of the retreat, I was able to write from my heart:

> *I am Bill Stevens, who has eros.*
> *Bill is truly human.*
> *Open the doors of your heart.*
> *Allow eros—pleasure—delight into your life.*

I could not let go of Diane. She lived in Georgia and was constantly in my thoughts. Of course, again, I brought this up in therapy. (It was good I never stopped to think what Gordon may have thought of me—I was so concerned about what everyone else thought—but never my therapist—how great is that?) The same thoughts obsessed me that I was being a bad person for having any sexual feelings and was harming her in some way because of this.

I wrote in my journal following my session with Gordon:

> *Why would you be using her if she is willing?*
> *There seems to be a fear of hurting the other.*
> *You shared and were totally accepted.*
> *She missed you and did not want to separate.*
> *Remember she cared for you—offered you her-self—her love.*

Diane wrote to me, and I wrote back to her. I felt strongly that God wanted to show his love for me through my relationship with her. But I did not want to use her in any negative way.

Gordon shared this with me:

> At your present sexual development, you find it possible to relate well with a 26-year-old woman. An older woman has so many experiences in relationships that you may not be able to relate well to yet.
>
> You seem more comfortable relating to women who need to be cared for. It is more difficult for you to relate to someone with their own identity. However, such a person as Diane can be a real companion. She will not be manipulative or possessive; this is not her need. If you enjoy each other's company and break through your self-sufficiency, something good can happen.

I went down to Georgia to visit Diane, who was beginning to live in a Christian Community there, and we spent a few days together. It was a goodbye. She later married a man in that community, and we gradually lost touch.

I never regretted either relationship, and it was interesting that I did not beat myself up for them. However, I was deeply saddened that this part of life was missed.

8

Reconnection

My Lord God,

I have no idea where I am going.

I do not see the road ahead of me.

I cannot know for certain where it will end.

Nor do I really know myself,

and the fact that I think I am following your will

does not mean I am actually doing so.

—*Thomas Merton*

On November 11, 1987, I wrote in my journal:

This part of my journey is over! It is clear. What is ahead, I do not know. My letter to the Provincial is my next step. In our dialogue, I will know what path to take. I am peaceful with whatever that path may be. The Lord has led me for the first 53 years of my life and will continue to do so.

I am so thankful this part of my journey is ending. Living with uncertainty, confusion, doubt, frustration, and inability to move forward is challenging. What an incredible journey I have been on. Only the Lord could have led me from one path to the next—leading me through circumstances, people, and events that I had no control over and were just right for me at the time. So many of these steps were almost too large for me but only possible to take by stretching my resources to the greatest extent.

There is no way I can list all the people involved in this journey—the role they have played is unbelievable. I cannot enumerate the number of people who reached out and supported me during this time. How good the Lord has been to me.

I do not have a lot of emotions when writing these thoughts down, but I have total conviction and peace inside of me, which indicates I have reached another turning point in my life. I can let go of the indecision; it is time to determine a new direction.

Two last elements holding me back from a final resolution were (1) a fear of being swallowed up once again by the Institution and (2) a fear that I might find a new relationship and regret my choice.

I am ready to write my letter to the Provincial, which I will do today. I am prepared to let go of the outcome being a certain way. I am peaceful—I have never thought I could be so peaceful at this time. I know the Lord is involved here and will let me know His plans *for me. I have done everything I could—followed every-thing these last 11 years to bring me to this point and now truly surrender to the Lord. I can do no more—it is in His hands—He must let me know His will. I can-not do anymore, but if I must remain in the darkness to accomplish your will—yes.*

And this is the letter I wrote to the province leader:

I want to share with you where I find myself at this point in my life and to indicate the direction I feel the Lord is calling me to follow.

Eleven years ago, during my last year in Schenec-tady, I realized I had to confront something in myself, but I did not understand what that was. That was the beginning of my recent journey, which has taken me on paths I never imagined I could walk.

Having come from a very rigid Catholic and some-what dysfunctional family into a very structured reli-gious life, I never knew or allowed myself to experience who Bill Stevens was. As a result, I embraced the iden-tity of "Brother" as my substitute and played this role well for thirty years.

I will never know how I had the strength to confront this in my life and take the initial step (in Boston) to let go of everything that had given me a sense of security and meaning. The Lord was leading me at this time by using people and events to bring me to the point of dis-satisfaction so that I would take this step without knowing where it would take me.

Over the past nine years, I have been in individual and group therapy on an almost weekly basis, have seen a spiritual director every month, and have spent many long and painful hours alone getting in touch with Bill Stevens.

This road has led me along many different paths: my clinical pastoral education, my leave of absence in Syracuse, my exclaustration in New Brunswick, my work experience in four different hospitals, my participation in the Erhard Seminars Training program (EST), my involvement in the Arthur Murray Dance Studio, my nine-month spiritual direction experience at the Center for Spirituality and Justice, and my working through two close relationships with women.

All of the above experiences and many others have been essential in helping me work through different feelings concerning my family and Congregation, and I have learned to accept and not be controlled by them. I need continued supervision in my growth, but the walls I built around myself have been broken, and the work has begun.

With more freedom than ever, I can choose what I want. It is very life-giving for me to realize that my choice can include being a member of the Congregation as Bill Stevens—one who can genuinely share his gifts and talents and not merely play the external "role of brother" to fulfill other people's expectations.

I need to put in words what my call to the Congregation means to me. It is an invitation by the Lord to Bill, who has all the limitations of a human being, to join a group of men who support each other in living a

Christian life and in responding to His call to bring the Good News of His love to others.

By my Vow of Poverty, I would share my gifts and talents with my brothers and those I serve and not be possessive of those things I use to perform my ministry and care for my needs. By my Vow of Obedience, I would pay attention to the direction in which the Lord is leading me by being aware of those things that bring me true happiness and peace and by sharing these desires with my Superiors so that the Lord's will for me can be discerned in the resulting dialogue. By my Vow of Chastity, I would seek to truly love my brothers, those whom I serve, and those who support me in my call, and I would work towards removing those barriers in myself that prevent this intimacy.

I am aware of a need to live alone at this time in my life to continue the healing process. The phrase "to live in community" elicits adverse reactions, which I have spent time with in prayer. I tried to "live in community" for over twenty-five years. For many reasons stemming from my personal and congregational history, I have often found the structure to be non-life-giving and detrimental to my emotional and spiritual growth.

As I continue my personal growth and become stronger in my identity, I will be able to live with others who share the same vision. However, "to live in community" means more to me than living within the walls of the same building. Community can be found by spending time with those brothers who are willing to support you and whom you experience as life-giving.

This letter is a request to reconnect as an active Congregation member. I want to continue my work at St. Peter's Medical Center, which I believe fulfills a need within the Church today and has been a source of spiritual and emotional growth. I want to remain in my apartment, which has been a blessing. Although challenging at times, the silence that comes from being alone has given me the space to confront myself and the opportunity to be more prayerful than at any other period of my life.

I want to use the income that I receive from my work to support myself and care for my needs, to continue my therapy, to pay pro-rata to the Congregation, and possibly commence studies towards a master's degree in divinity at Princeton Theological Seminary on a part-time basis.

I have recently been elected Representative of New Jersey for this region of the National Association of Catholic Chaplains, have become strongly involved with a Catholic community with whom I worship on Sunday, and have been developing a network of friends along with a group of brothers who have been supportive of my journey. I have been trying to demonstrate concretely for myself the possibility of living the life of a Christian Brother as Bill Stevens.

I need a sense of belonging to something, support and affirmation, and a sense of home and brotherhood. I am aware of my "brokenness" and desire to share this with my brothers to help us both become whole. I have shared with you my needs, desires, and vision, and now I need to know if these are compatible with the vision and direction of the Province.

I frequently think of a quote attributed to Thomas Merton during his last days in the United States. He said, "The supreme reward in a religious community should be that a man or woman be set free for what they desire most." That is what I am asking. Something deep within me tells me the Lord has led me along this path of healing for a purpose, and He will give me the strength to be open to His will for me as it is made known.

I mailed the letter and was eventually accepted back into the brotherhood. I remained in my ministry in New Jersey, living alone. Although my living situation continued to be an issue addressed frequently over the next few years, which became exhausting and a bit frustrating, the bottom line was they cared for me as a person and supported my ministry a hundred percent. Permissions were granted in my ministry and living, I could not have asked for anything more.

The Road Ahead

My Lord God,
I have no idea where I am going.
I do not see the road ahead of me.
I cannot know for certain where it will end.
Nor do I really know myself,
and the fact that I think I am following your will
does not mean I am actually doing so.

But I believe the desire to please you, does in fact please you. And I hope to have that desire in all that I am doing.

I hope that I will never do anything apart from that desire. And I know if I do this, you will lead me by the right road, though I might know nothing about it.

Therefore will I trust you always though I may seem lost. And in the shadow of death, I will not fear, for you are forever with me, and you will never leave me to face my troubles alone.

—Thomas Merton

9

AIDS

You begin by just being
who you are

A loving, caring, whole
person

Created in my image

Whose special light of love

Happens to shine on men,

As I intended for you.

— *John Fortunato*, Embracing the Exile

When I walked into the room of my first AIDS patient in the late 80s at St. Peter's Medical Center, I had a reaction deep inside my body. My CPE training told me to pay attention. During this time, when a person entered the hospital with a diagnosis of AIDS, it was a death sentence. I was physically there, but barely. I wanted to turn and run out of the room. I became aware of my fear and sense of powerlessness. I somehow fumbled through the visit but knew I was not truly present or pastoral. I could not get out of the room fast enough. So, I sat with the experience for a long time. If I was to continue this ministry, I had to get help. I had to educate myself.

Before getting that help, I had another encounter with a person with AIDS who had come into the hospital. I will call him Bob. He was married with two sons. He and his wife decided to keep his diagnosis secret from not only his two sons but also all his relatives, except Bob's father. This included the parish priest, where one of his sons attended school. This kind of decision was not uncommon at that time. I worked with him for several months, visited him often at his home, and tried to support his wife, whose coping mechanisms were being stretched by the secrecy. She could never share her story with anyone, nor was Bob able to do so. All that people were told was he had cancer and nothing more could be done for him.

Bob became very depressed and lost all his desire to fight his illness. He wanted to die. He could not bear living the lie any longer. He literally gave his life to keep his story a secret. As the end drew near, I asked him if there was anything he would like to say to his family and friends at his funeral. I said I would read anything he would like to write down. He thought about it for some time, and then, one day, he dictated to me his final thoughts. Ironically, the parish priest initially said nobody could get up and speak at the funeral mass. Only after much intervention did he reluctantly let me talk for a few moments at the end of the service.

I did not tell his family beforehand about his last thoughts, so they were surprised, and it was also meaningful. They were very grateful to hear him express his love and appreciation, and of course, they asked me for a copy of the letter at the end of the service—something they would cherish.

Shortly after, I did seek help from the only outreach organization in the state of New Jersey at the time— the Hyacinth Foundation, an organization founded by gay men to care for gay men and to educate everyone about this disease. So I went and educated myself about AIDS and, in the process, went through their buddy training program as well, and submitted my name to be considered as a volunteer to be a buddy to someone with AIDS. Well, this transformed my life. I was never to be the same again.

I was assigned to Leonce. He was a gay man from Texas and addicted to drugs. He had recently lost both his parents. His sister was living in New Jersey, and he came to live with her.

Leonce became my teacher. I learned about his life and the pain of losing ALL his friends to the disease. (Pause and take that in.) I learned about enabling and being manipulated and about the pain of addiction. Amazingly, Leonce was determined to become clean before he died, to find a relationship, to become an actor, to come out publicly to make a difference, to fight stigmatization, and to educate kids about the epidemic and how to be safe. Quite an agenda after being dealt this hand.

It was not always a straight line from beginning to end. But life is that way. He landed from Texas with a dog and a bag and somehow got a ride to his sister's place. We met for the first time on April 20, 1988. He was still using. He found night work at a local industry. Yes, I gave him money when he needed it and sheltered him when he needed it. There were times when I felt he was conning me, and my whole body told me something else was going on than what was playing out in front of me. I had to learn from my mistakes, too.

I know I fell in love with Leonce. It was not mutual. I once shared my feelings with Leonce in a letter, and he wrote back:

> I know I may be a fool, and I know you can make me happy, and no one has ever treated me like you have. But I do not have the same feelings that you have for me.

What beautiful honesty.

But something was awakened in my 55-year-old body.

In my journal, I wrote a passage from the book *Embracing the Exile* by John Fortunato:

> To be gay and Christian, integrating both into the wholeness we deep down know ourselves to be, to embrace them both as gifts of God and to live our lives authentically, rejoicing in those gifts as part of the uniqueness that makes us who we are, is to place ourselves on the outskirts of the community we most care about. It's beyond the realm of our choice. Exile is where we find ourselves

when we are who we are. It's most often a hard place to be. . . .

How can love be wrong? It all comes from me. I made you whole. You're my son. Nothing can separate you from my love. I redeemed you before the beginning of time. In my Father's house, there is a mansion waiting just for you.

I've given you gifts. Share them. I've given you light. Lighten the world. I empower you with my love. Love them.

But they call my light darkness. They call my love perverted. They call my gifts corruption. What are you asking me to do?

Love them anyway. Love them anyway.

But how?

You begin by just being who you are—a loving, caring, whole person created in my image, whose special light of love happens to shine on men, as I intended for you.

You must speak your pain and affirm the wholeness I have made you to be when they assail it. You must protest when you are treated as less than a child of mine.

(This incredible book placed being gay in such a positive way it overwhelmed me and gave me the courage to entertain the possibility that this was who I was, which was quite the opposite of words like "intrinsically evil" used by Cardinal Ratzinger).

10

Fully Embracing Who I Am

*I myself shall pasture my
sheep, I myself shall give
them rest . . . I shall look for
the lost one, bring back the
stray, bandage the injured,
and make the sick strong.
. . . I shall be a true shepherd
to them.*

I wrote in my journal in July 1986 that I was looking for a spiritual director who could receive information without judgment or advice, be present, share my journey, and suggest questions to ask myself during this journey. Kathy Begley was my answer, and she was to be my spiritual director and most valued companion for the next 37 years.

In the summer of 1991, I went on an eight-day retreat with Kathy. It was an annual event I had put into my life at that time because of its profound benefits. During the retreat, I signed up to do one of the readings during the daily liturgy that was part of our days together. I did not look at the reading beforehand. This is what I read. It was from Ezekiel 34: 1-18.

> God's message came to me: Son of Man prophecy against the Shepherd—leaders of Israel. Yes, prophesy! Tell those shepherds, "God, the Master, says: Doom to you shepherds of Israel, feeding your own mouths. Aren't shepherds supposed to feed the sheep? You drink the milk, you make clothes from the wool, you roast the lambs, but you don't feed the sheep. You don't build up the weak ones, don't heal the sick, don't doctor the injured, don't go after the strays, don't look for the lost. You bully and badger them. And now they are scattered every which way because there was no shepherd—scattered and easy pickings for wolves and coyotes. Scattered—my sheep!— exposed and vulnerable across mountains and hills. My sheep scattered all over the world, and no one looking out for them!
>
> Therefore, shepherds, listen to the message of God: As sure as I am the living God—Decree of God, the Master—because my sheep have been turned into mere prey, into easy meals for wolves because you shepherds ignored them and only fed yourselves, listen to what God has to say:
>
> Watch out! I am coming down on the shepherds and taking my sheep back. They're fired as shepherds of my sheep. No more shepherds who just feed themselves! I'll rescue my sheep from their greed. They're not going to feed off my sheep any longer!

God, the Master, says: From now on, I myself am the Shepherd. I'm looking for them. I'm going after my sheep as shepherds go after their flocks when they get scattered. I'll rescue them from the places they've been scattered to in the storms. I'll bring them back from foreign peoples, gather them from foreign countries, and bring them back to their home country. I'll feed them on the mountains of Israel. Along the streams, among their own people. I'll lead them into lush pastures so they can roam the mountain pastures of Israel, graze at leisure, and feed in the rich pastures on the mountains of Israel. And I myself will be the Shepherd of my sheep; I myself will make sure they get plenty of rest. I'll go after the lost. I'll collect the strays, I'll doctor the injured, I'll build up the weak ones so they're not exploited.

I had heard of conversion experiences and God breaking into people's lives, but at the age of fifty-eight and in my forty-first year of religious life, such a God was foreign to me. I was in desperate need of internal healing but knew in my heart that nothing so good could happen to me, and I even doubted that such things occurred to others.

However, my miracle happened during that eight-day directed retreat in the silence of beautiful August summer days. I received the precious gift to totally love and accept myself as the gay person whom God created me to be. After over forty years of self-hate and shame, the True Shepherd leapt from the pages of Ezekiel 34 to rescue me from the mouths of those who would want me to believe I am an abomination of my Creator. This True Shepherd bandaged my wounds and made me strong. I was now part of the flock.

My True Shepherd touched my life and invited me through my spiritual director to be under His care in rich pastures. My retreat guidelines were:

> Get in touch with who you are and bring that person into the presence of God; from all eternity, God has chosen this time to be with you; all you need to do is show up and let go of any expectations.

Early in the retreat, it became clear to me that I was being asked to know who I was in my deepest being and to accept that God had created me as a gay man.

One morning, I was so in touch with my body I experienced it as something beautiful and good—with sexual and alive feelings. All was good, and God was present.

Later that day, it felt so right that my body was good and I was an instrument for giving and receiving love. I knew it was time to turn one's back to the violent Church and not listen to this voice—it is not the voice of God. The Shepherd's voice gives life, peace, and hope and is not destructive of nature. "I have come that you might have life and live it fully."

I listened for the guilt and the fear to return, but they were absent. Only feelings of peace and joy remained. My deepest wound is revealed to me: I DID NOT BELIEVE ANYONE, INCLUDING GOD, COULD LOVE ME FOR MYSELF.

I have always felt I was a bad person because of my sexual desires, sexual thoughts, and masturbation.

I have put up a wall around me to keep people away, including my God. I am in desperate need of healing.

I desperately need to be touched, skin against skin, and feel the warmth of another human being in my life.

This is the most profound need of a human being deprived of all human touch and human warmth for fifty-five years.

It is the desperate cry of one who can no longer keep human beings out of his life. This is not about sexuality or celibacy but breathing life into a dying body. This is where my healing lies.

We all need to receive God's love, no matter what it looks like.

"I myself shall pasture my sheep, I myself shall give them rest. . . . I shall look for the lost one, bring back the stray, bandage the injured, and make the sick strong. . . . I shall be a True Shepherd to them."

—*Freedom Glorious Freedom*

REFLECTIONS ON THE CASE HISTORY (by John McNeill)

My client continued on his healing path since that retreat. He has come out to his family and his religious order, and he is actively seeking out gay friends and companions. In many ways, this very moving case is unique, as is the person whose history it is. At the same time, however, it reveals the same basic pattern of recovery that many of my clients, especially those from a strong religious background, have had to pass through in order to succeed in coming out of the closet, positively accepting their gayness, and laying the foundation for a healthy gay relationship. One cannot find a healthy relationship on an aspect of self one hates and is ashamed of.

The first step in the typical process is the interiorization of the homophobia of family, Church, and culture. In the past, this almost always led to the feeling of being different and the only one in the world with these feelings. This, in turn, leads to a total suppression of one's gay identity, using pathological religious concepts of fear and shame to achieve that repression.

Having suppressed all feelings, the individual tries to live "out of the head," developing conflict-free intellectual skills and burying themselves in their studies and work. They base their identity on their ability to meet the needs of others while repressing and denying their own needs. Many from a Catholic background will, frequently unconsciously, use a vocation to celibate religious life to avoid having to deal at all with sexuality and intimacy. Sooner or later, this process of self-denial and repression will bottom out with serious depression, rage, and, on frequent occasions, serious alcohol or drug abuse, compulsive acting out of needs for intimacy, affection, and sexual fulfillment leading to greater shame, guilt, and fear, sometimes resulting in psychological breakdown and even efforts at suicide.

The client, in this case history, bottomed out with serious depression, which led him to take the courageous action of seeking out individual and group therapy, fortunately with a gay-positive therapist. He also had the good fortune to be aware that secular therapy alone would not be adequate to meet his needs. He also had to find a way to mature spiritually.

Through competent spiritual directors, he began learning how to discern spirits and hear the voice of God speaking to him in his heart directly through his experiences and feelings. He started the process of sorting out his pathological religious feelings from his healthy, mature experience of God's love for him. He began building a healthy religious relationship with the God of love. He had to risk taking distance from the Institutional Church's authority to achieve that growth.

My client had to go through several years of healing psychotherapy and spiritual direction before he was ready to address the issue of his gay identity safely. This breakthrough occurred for him when he fell in love with a man with AIDS for whom he was a buddy. The deep peace and joy he experienced in that love was his first step toward a positive acceptance of his gayness.

But the struggle to heal the wound of his self-hatred was not over. At every step of the process, my client sought God's help through prayer, retreats, and spiritual direction. He made a wise application of the

*saying of Ignatius. We must pray as if everything de-
pended on us. We must act as if everything depended
on God.*

I appreciate John McNeill's incredible support over
five years. He made time for me despite the many
things with which he was involved. His ability to listen,
offer counsel, and loving support changed my life.

I seldom write poetry. But if something touches me
deeply, it is how I process it. I will close this chapter
with a poem I wrote one day during my last year of
seeing John McNeill. I would always go over to New
York early and had found a small breakfast place close
to his office. I would sit there for a couple of hours,
journal, and prepare for my visit. But it was more than
that; it was a sacred space and had become my church.
They knew me when I walked in; when I sat down, they
knew what to bring me without asking. They respected
my space and let me stay as long as I wanted. Then, one
day:

THE WRONG STREET

*I came by, and you were not there
Is this not the street?
"This store is for rent."
Did I make a wrong turn?
Where are the muffins in the window?
The open door?
The warm greeting?
My coffee, juice, and muffin — without my saying a
word*

Even when my last visit was so long ago.

With eight million people in New York, why was I so
special?
You never made me feel rushed
No one else stayed as long
I felt you would let me stay all day
You just wanted me to feel safe, comfortable, and served.

You never knew you made this my church, did you?
You never knew I often came in pain and confusion, did
you?
And I wrote, and I wrote, and I wrote
And shed many quiet tears.
Why was I given this oasis?
You never knew how grateful I was, did you?
How could I tell you what your simple actions did for
me?

How many other lives did you touch?
Accepting all, no matter what their status.
Over the years, I noticed your
Welcoming, acknowledging, serving, caring.
It wasn't about money; it was about decent human love.
But you are not there now because of money.
The rent would not stop rising.

The sign read, "We will miss you."
You have no idea how much I will miss you, do you?
And because of the missing, I have had to find this oasis
deep inside me.

♠ Bill Stevens ♠

In your very departure, you have left me a gift I can always carry with me.

I must be on the wrong street . . .

11

The Office of Pastoral Care for People with AIDS in the Diocese of Metuchen

To respond to the HIV/AIDS crisis within the Diocese, by creating outreach programs which concretely demonstrate that people affected by the disease do not walk alone.

One day, as I was walking around St. Peter's Medical Center, I met Fr. Joe, whom I had met before, and he shared with me the Bishop's intentions to create an Office of Pastoral Care for People Living with AIDS. Something moved within me as soon as the words were out of his mouth, and I knew that would be my next job. It happened that quickly. The rest I trusted would play itself out.

I created a timetable for myself:

10/27: Tell Fr. Joe of my interest and ask him to assemble a package including salary, benefits, housing, and job description.

11/11 Tell John Matuska, President of SPMC (Sr. Marie de Pazzi had died), and the pastoral care staff about my applying for the position and ask Fr. Joe to get back to me before Thanksgiving when I hand in my resignation.

12/1–12/21 Tell my landlady I will be leaving—giving her a month's notice—pack and move into a new residence

12/21–1/1—vacation in CA with my sister and nephew

1/4–1/26 Make a renewal retreat at Christ the King Retreat House in Syracuse

1/26–1/31 Final Preparations

2/1 Start new job

Of course, a letter to my Province Leader would be the first hurdle. Again, the issue of living alone was brought up as an issue, and I needed to address it.

11/20/88

The contents of your letter took me totally by surprise as I did not feel my present living situation and min-

istry in the Diocese of Metuchen would become an issue. It was not my recollection from my meeting with
you, upon choosing to return from exclaustration,
that you were placing a limit upon my ministry in the
Diocese of Metuchen. On the contrary, you were very
positive about it, and I felt as if I had been missioned
to do the work of the Founder here. In my meeting
with the Visitor last year, this issue was never
brought up, and I have no recollection of this coming
up in any conversation with you these past two years.

When you quote our constitutions to me that
"brotherhood and community is the principal source
of our companionship and the privileged context for
our personal growth," I sense you feel I am not making this part of my life. Although I may not be tradi-
tionally experiencing community and brotherhood,
I do find brotherhood from a group of brothers
who have supported me, and this is my community at
present. I reach out to them regularly, which has been
a privileged context for my personal growth.

Five years ago, when I took exclaustration, the central issue was living in one of our communities. It
was brought up to me every year until I took the step
of exclaustration because I could not in conscience respond the way I was being asked to. I did not feel I
was being asked to make this choice when I returned
two years ago, but apparently, it was part of your
agenda, but I did not hear it.

I am presently the Regional Director of the National Association of Catholic Chaplains for the States
of New Jersey and Pennsylvania; I have been elected

to the steering committee of the State AIDS Interfaith Network; I am a member of the Middlesex County AIDS Coalition and Chairperson of their Ad Hoc Housing Committee which is close to establishing a house for children with AIDS in the county and will be working to develop other residences for adults living with AIDS. I am an active volunteer (in the buddy program and speaker's bureau) in the Hyacinth Foundation, a statewide non-profit volunteer group formed to support persons living with AIDS and their families. All of this, I believe, makes me an excellent candidate for the position of Director of Pastoral Care for People Living with AIDS, as I have established good working relationships and a trust level with these different groups, which will make it that much easier to truly work with them in creating complementary programs of service.

I do not perceive these activities as "postponing my return to community living" but as responding to the needs of the Church as I see it in my life at this time. I have negotiated for a residence to be part of this office so that a spiritual center can be established for people living with AIDS and those who support them. I can envision a community of people supporting each other in this work. I want to call it Edmund House, for I believe Edmund Rice would have had such a place if this disease had been prevalent in his time.

New Jersey ranks fourth in the nation after New York, California, and Florida in the number of adults who have developed AIDS and second behind New York in affected children. Of the 5,300 cases of AIDS in New Jersey since 1982, 58% of them have died. The projected statistics for 1991 are overwhelming. Bishop Hughes is one of the few New Jersey bishops who seems concerned and willing to do more than pay lip service to the crisis.

Since you feel living in one of our existing communities is something the Lord is asking you to confront me with, I need to respect your wishes and deal with the question. However, it is essential for me to avoid dealing with this annually and to be made to feel I am less of a brother until I live in one of our existing communities.

Father Szulwach will present my name to the Bishop as his replacement at his meeting on Wednesday, November 30. I would like to have my status clarified by that time.

Province leadership and the Bishop approved everything. I was quite excited about it. To start my ministry with the diocese would be a real shot in the arm. I had been in direct hospital ministry for almost ten years, and to use the experiences from this work for my ministry to people struggling with AIDS just seemed right for me. It was building the ministry from scratch, although Fr. Joe Szulwach had begun to make the office known to some parishes and had a handful of volunteers helping him.

Shortly after I started my ministry in the diocese, the bishop gave me a house in St. Mary's Parish in Perth Amboy, NJ, where I could live. It was previously a convent for a nearby high school, which had closed. This school was then turned into a diocesan center that would house both the Office of Social Ministries and the AIDS ministry.

So, I named the residence Edmund House. A friend, Jean Potter, who worked in the social ministries office and would become a close friend for many years after, made a beautiful plaque in calligraphy inscribing a brief history of our founder. She also jumped in to help me fix up and paint many sections of the house. I will always be deeply grateful to her for that support.

One of the first things I did was to publish a statement about the purpose of the office:

> *To respond to the HIV/AIDS crisis within the diocese by creating outreach programs which concretely demonstrate that people affected by the disease do not walk alone.*

Then I began to establish various outreach programs for the AIDS community. Fr. Joseph Szulwach was very supportive of the office. It was his baby, and he was very instrumental in opening all sorts of avenues with the priests in the diocese who would support its activities. We formed an advisory council with these priests and met regularly to formulate goals and check on our progress.

One of the first things I did was to become involved in all the AIDS coalitions in the different counties of the diocese, letting them know who we were and what we were about and being open to taking on positions within these groups. At the same time, I was trying to address needs that other service groups were not addressing. So, I enrolled in a massage school in Princeton called Health Choices Center for the Healing Arts and became a Certified Massage Practitioner. I later became certified in reflexology and completed a Level I Reiki practitioner program.

People with AIDS were very isolated with this disease; they became the lepers of the 20th century. Many had lesions on their skin (purple blotches), which could appear on their face, legs, and arms, which only further isolated them. Families and friends disowned them. Many churches discriminated against them. Since AIDS was connected to sex and drugs, judgments were made, and sufferers were excluded. So just offering the services of massage and Reiki spoke volumes.

12

Coming Out to Family

The truth
Is
Belligerent
It slithers
Into our lives.

Or it
Explodes our world
We do not
Control it.

The truth
Is all knowing
And cannot
Be contained.

— Raven 6/5/23

Almost from the beginning of my time with Kathy, she always encouraged me to pay attention to the moment, for that is where I would find God. And notice what gave me life. This happened to me as I began volunteering with the Hyacinth Foundation and became a buddy to Leonce. Something awoke within me, and I could now put a name on it. I never could before. The name I always gave to it was sin, the name was guilt, the name was bad. But I began to realize I am gay; I am a homosexual. Now, what does that mean?

As indicated earlier, I took some time off after leaving St. Peter's Medical Center and starting my new work with the diocese. I did visit my sister in California and spent almost a month in Syracuse at Christ the King Retreat House in a DeMello renewal program led by Fr. Jim Dolan.

I also went on a three-day retreat in Bangor, PA, at Kirkridge Retreat House. It was a retreat for gay men given by John McNeill, a Jesuit who was prophetic and spoke out strongly for the rights and dignity of gay men within the institutional church and paid a huge price for doing it.

So it was during this two-month sabbatical that I spent a lot of time sitting with this whole question of my sexuality, and I decided to share my gayness with some close friends and some family members. I did not need to make any big public announcements but felt a need to make it real for myself, and this was a way to do that.

On one of my trips to California, I met my nephew, Tommy, and realized that he was in a gay relationship. We did not speak much about it then, but I was accepting of it and delighted that he could take this journey despite the incredible obstacles and risks involved in the 70's and 80's. He was a hero to me. His uncle should be a model for him, but he was modeling for me the courage and integrity it takes to be true to yourself.

So he was one of the people I wanted to share my coming out with, and I wrote him a letter. He responded:

1/12/89

Dear Bergin,

I feel privileged that you chose to share the process of coming out with me. Although, in my usual compulsive fashion, I would choose to immediately share my personal experiences with you, I sense that, at this point, that wouldn't be of assistance to you. I am so happy that you went to the seminar with John McNeill. His name rings a bell, from where, I don't know.

Ironically, you mention my courage. It is you who have given me the courage to forge on towards my goal of being in the helping professions. Before I became aware of how you and Agnes made a difference in the world, I felt that coming from a dysfunctional family possibly precluded one's ability to offer counseling. Your courage and what you stand for have helped me through all my considerations as to why I can't do those things.

I could, if you like, be a resource should you want to have access to the names of bookstores in LA or NYC that would have much literature that may be of interest. As well, my library may have books to interest you.

The memories that I do have of coming out harken to a very exciting, stimulating time of self-love and self-discovery—the joys outweigh the pains. Fortunately, the few pains I did experience were from the outside, not from myself.

I shared it with my sister Agnes on my trip to California and also wrote my brother Edward in Boston, and he responded:

> *Dear Bergin,*
> *Thank you for your letter of 1/9 from the retreat house in Syracuse.*
> *I am delighted that you had a profitable retreat with John McNeill in the Poconos. I saw him interviewed on the Larry King show only two weeks ago. I know that the fact that the R.C. Church is so rigid about sexual matters in general and homosexual matters in particular must have added immeasurably to your conflicts and sufferings about feelings over which you have no control. I hope that you will enjoy increasingly deeper peace in this area of your life.*
> *I must confess I do not regard it as a big deal. Feelings are feelings, and we have no choice but to accept them. Pheme likes sweet potatoes, and I like white potatoes, and neither of us is ever going to change. Fortunately, we have never been condemned as human beings for having these feelings. That's what is so unfair and vicious about the R.C. Church's condemnation of people for having these feelings.*
> *You show good judgment in sharing this with only a small circle. The religious nut cakes of the world are incapable of really hearing anything you might want to share about this. And you can do more for gays by quiet action than by provoking irrational reactions and confrontations.*
> *Anyway, whose business is it? Except for the Phil Donohue and Oprah shows, people don't talk about*

their sexual proclivities. We all have our little favorite
sexual deals, but it's private, right?
Good luck with your continuing transitional work!
Love,
Edward

I knew they would be supportive before I shared this with them, but receiving their responses meant everything to me.

13

Beginnings of
Chrysalis Ministry

*Panel speakers, priests,
and religious with AIDS
literally wore paper bags
over their heads for fear that
their bishop or religious
superior would know who
they were.*

Much of my ministry attempted to create safe spaces for people to come out of isolation, gather, and support each other. I heard of a man in Washington D.C. named Lou Tesconi. Lou was a lawyer from Texas who was earning a six-figure income and had a thriving practice but paid attention to a call within him to join the Carmelites. At 36, he sold his practice and everything he had and gave all the proceeds to charity. He joined the Carmelites and went to Washington to begin his novitiate year. During his novitiate year, he received a diagnosis of Kaposi sarcoma, an AIDS-related cancer, at 2 pm. By 8 am the following day, he was asked to leave.

He did not know what to do with his life. He still felt called to ministry. A few weeks later, in November 1986, Lou attended a pastoral workshop on AIDS, which the Washington Archdiocese sponsored. In the middle of the workshop, when there was a discussion about AIDS and the needs of those affected, Lou stood up in the middle of the 250 priests and nuns and asked, "When are we going to start seeing it as ministering to our own?" It was a conversation-stopper. But two people came to him after the meeting, a Catholic priest from Catholic Charities and a woman Catholic activist and psychologist, who challenged him to do something independently. With their support and encouragement, he moved forward and never looked back. He created Damien Ministries.

He was a very gifted and talented man with great compassion. He did two quite extraordinary things. One was holding a yearly conference for priests and religious who had AIDS and for leaders in religious congregations and dioceses to learn how to support them. I attended one of these conferences, and I was shocked to see the panel speakers, priests, and religious with AIDS literally wearing paper bags over their heads for fear that their bishop or religious superior would know who they were. They shared their stories and challenged communities to open their hearts to their own.

I got to know Lou, and he told me about four-day retreat programs he was running for people with AIDS who came from all parts of the United States. He held them at a retreat house in Washington. For anyone who wished to attend, he paid all their expenses for the retreat and their travel through fundraising programs. One unique fundraiser was to send a direct letter to the priests of the diocese to request their support.

In April 1989, Lou invited me to attend one of his retreats.

> *Dear Bill*
>
> *Thank you for your recent letter regarding our retreat program for people living with AIDS.*
>
> *I would be very interested in discussing providing a retreat in your area sometime during 1990 as a collaborative venture. As you know, this year we are taking our retreats "on the road," with programs taking place in New Orleans, Chicago, and New York City.*
>
> *In any event, I have added your name to the list for the September 11–14 program here in the Washington area. You will receive registration materials in early August.*
>
> *If you ever find yourself in the Washington area, please pray with our community any weekday at 8:15.*
>
> *Best regards,*
> *Louis Tesconi, Executive Director*

During that retreat, I met many people from New Jersey, and I wondered why they should have to travel this distance to attend such a retreat and why something similar could not happen closer to home.

These encounters with Lou Tesconi and my participation in his program were life-changing. I asked Lou if he would help me set up a similar program in New Jersey. I also began talking about it with Fr. Joe and the local parish priest where I lived.

In April 1990, I contacted three people who came together with me in Paterson, NJ, to talk about our first retreat—Fr. Angelo Gambatese from Paterson, Fr. Damien Charboneau from Perth Amboy, and Sr. Helen Bearisto from Highland Park. We needed to find a place to hold the retreat. We contacted Sr. Carol Heller at Xavier Center on the grounds of St. Elizabeth College in Morristown, NJ.

Sr. Carol immediately opened the doors of Xavier Center to us. It was an incredibly generous offer. Such a decision could have repercussions, and Sr. Carol had to do her homework and educate and prepare her staff for our arrival. There was much fear and ignorance about HIV, and many retreat houses were hesitant to risk taking such a step. We were always profoundly grateful for Sr. Carol's vision, courage, and integrity in creating a living chrysalis for the team and our participants.

As an example of the tangible fear of AIDS at that time, we later contacted another retreat house to hold a retreat. The director was very positive, and we sent a couple of our team members to educate the staff at the retreat house. But before we came on the retreat, the housekeeping staff gave notice they would not be there. After the retreat, all the bedding had to be thrown out before they would return to their duties. This exemplifies the deep fear present in society at the time and further underlines the fearlessness of Sr. Carol Heller in doing what was right despite the risk of people choosing to no longer come to the retreat house when they became aware of her decision.

So Lou came with three members of his team. In addition to those who attended the meeting in April, nine other professionals from different spiritual traditions already involved in direct AIDS ministry in NJ offered their services—Carol Bamesberger; Mary Capron; Br. Tom Cunningham, a Holy Cross brother; Fr. James Lloyd; Sr. Mary McGrath; Michael Nelson, RN; Carol O'Neill, RN; and Fr. Phil Rotunno. And our first retreat became a reality.

Lou died at the age of 41, thirteen months later. He accomplished an incredible amount in the five years following his diagnosis. He created the first outreach program for AIDS in Washington. He formed a community of men living with AIDS to serve those in need—those in prison, those who were homeless, and those whose families and friends abandoned them. In August 1987 he created the first housing unit in the United States for women living with AIDS. In December 1987 he created a housing unit for men living with AIDS, and in September 1991, he created a third unit for Hispanic men. It was through his actions that he educated communities on how to care for those living with AIDS and how to support their families and loved ones. Although never ordained, he was indeed a priest to countless people, and his ministry continues to this day in Washington. I am deeply indebted to Lou for inspiring me in my ministry.

14

The Life and Death of
Two Special People

A friend is a reflection of
God's Love.
— Rose

I met Rose at a support group at Sacred Heart
Church in New Brunswick, NJ. As part of the Office
of Pastoral Care program, we sought to create
support groups within the church community and give
parishioners the opportunity to become involved in
outreach to people living with AIDS. The pastor had a
group from his church make a luncheon for us each
week, which helped create a beautiful, caring environment.

This group was made up mainly from a nearby
Methadone clinic for those struggling with drug addiction. In addition, since AIDS was a blood-borne virus, it
was transmitted easily by sharing needles and, therefore, spread into the drug community. Many women
became infected either because of their own use of
drugs or contracting it from their husbands. So New

Jersey was one of the first states to see large numbers of infected women and children.

Tom Cronin, a counselor from the Methadone clinic, ran the group. Joan deVelder, a social worker from Planned Parenthood, worked with him to create various activities and listen to people's concerns. We encouraged people from the group to participate in all the available activities. We always tried to support them in attending the state-wide retreat programs run by Chrysalis Ministry.

It was a unique group. Each person had their own story. And Tom taught us the do's and don't's in working with a person with an addiction. They were great people, but many were con artists because this is how they survived on the streets. They were good at it. I had learned many hard lessons and still was often caught. Tom was so good at calling them on it.

No matter how hard you try, one person always wins your heart and soul. And Rose was that person for me. She had an incredible story and was determined to be her own person and live life as fully as possible. She would stick up for herself and all people living with the virus. She would not let people put her down. She worked at a supermarket in the meat department in town. When the store discovered she had AIDS and wanted to fire her, she would have none of that. They compromised; they let her go but paid her salary. This worked out fine because she was beginning to develop more health issues at the time. One of her coworkers, Joe, was so impressed with her that he invited her to live in his home because of her finances and the fact that he knew she was living alone and developing more debilitating symptoms. She was just that kind of person; she touched people deeply.

She had always wanted a red convertible. One day, towards the end of her illness, Rose cashed in everything she owned, bought a red convertible, and began riding around in it. Joe got right on top of it and was able to bring it back to the dealer and get her old car back. He always looked after her.

She was able to come to several of our state-wide retreat programs and then began to have hospitalizations due to complications of her disease. I had planned to see my sister in California during Christmas '92 and knew Rose was not doing well when I was about to leave. It was hard for me to go, but I did. Later, the secretary at the office told me Rose had called the office before she died, looking for me. I told her I was leaving, but she could not comprehend that fully. I got a call on December 24, 1992, in California that she had died.

The next day, I wrote a eulogy, which I would deliver a few weeks later at a memorial service:

> *A 36-year-old woman died of AIDS yesterday, the mother of two children and a grandmother — another statistic.*
>
> *A woman whose life dramatically changed at the age of 9 when her mother died — her father abandoning her to take care of her grandmother.*
>
> *Her life was never the same. It led to teenage pregnancy and early drug use with its inevitable results — crime and jail.*

Society would like to say—well, she asked for it. What can you expect? She deserves what she got.

Did she really?

She was diagnosed with AIDS while in solitary confinement in jail. Did she deserve that?

When she shared this with her family after leaving prison, they wanted nothing to do with her. Did she deserve that?

When she shared it with her best friend, that friend abandoned her. Did she deserve that?

They told her to leave her job when she shared the diagnosis where she worked. Did she deserve that?

When she shared it with her dentist, he told her to go someplace else. Did she deserve that?

What did she offer the world in return?

She courageously lived her life fully with the AIDS virus. Did we deserve that?

She freed herself from her drug addiction through a methadone treatment program. Did we deserve that?

She became a leader in a support group for others in recovery and living with the virus. Did we deserve that?

She spoke out publicly about her disease so that others would be aware. Did we deserve that?

She spoke passionately to youth groups to make them aware of her mistakes and begged them to make different choices. Did we deserve that?

She made amends to all her family members and friends. Did they deserve that?

She is more than a statistic.

The person cast aside by our society did not accept the message given to her. She became the messenger, leaving us with a message from which we cannot hide.

She used all the misfortunes of her life to grow and become a fully human person — a feat that few people reach in twice her lifespan. She completed all her tasks, was loved by those who knew her as a person, and was admired for her courage, strength, love, and dedication to letting people know the terrible tragedy of abandoning those who have become ravaged by a virus.

Yes, a 36-year-old woman died of AIDS yesterday. The tragedy is society never knew what a priceless human being she was.

In a previous chapter in this memoir, I spoke a little bit about Leonce. I focused on his struggles and lapses, all part of his recovery process. But I would like to share with you more of his story, and I will steal a beautiful description of this from a book written by Katherine Fair Connelly entitled *Recovering from the Loss of a Loved One to AIDS — Help for Surviving Family, Friends, and Lovers Who Grieve*. She used the experiences of real people and interviewed several people for this book, and Leonce was one of those. I will use excerpts from her book:

> In a tragic and uncanny twist of fate, Leonce Chabernaud's parents died two weeks apart— each on their birthday! Leonce was only nineteen. His mother had been fighting cancer, but a heart

attack ended that battle. His father died of cirrhosis of the liver. The young man was utterly devastated by the double loss.

Leonce shared how difficult it was for him when he was living in New York to continue to lose the newly made friends there.

"I had left our home in Texas and was living in New York at Bailey House, a hospice for people with AIDS. Although I tried not to get close to anyone there, when you have three meals a day together, you get to know who and how they are. I was devastated when so many of them died. When I first started losing the friends I had made there, I was getting sober from drugs and alcohol."

One particular friend had a profound effect on Leonce and triggered a strong emotional response.

"In my first year and a half at Bailey House, Ron lived right next to me. Each person had a room to himself. We became good friends. One day, Ron made a conscious decision to die at Bailey House instead of a hospital. I thought this decision was wonderful but also very hard for me. I visited Ron every day and would sleep next to him in a chair at night. He was the nearest thing to my family that I had. One night, it hit me between the eyes that Ron wouldn't be around much longer. He had stopped eating, stopped his medication, and stopped doing the things that were keeping him alive. That night, I stayed in my room. I was crying out very loudly, sobbing. I didn't mean to make a spectacle of myself. All the people at Bailey House were aware of what was going on. The next day, Ron died."

After his friend's death, Leonce found it impossible to remain at Bailey House and made efforts through his case worker to be moved to an independent housing unit through the AIDS Resource Center. "My case worker helped me make the change to the Scattered Site Program, which runs Bailey House but also runs this program for people with AIDS who want to live on their own and think they can handle it. I stayed in one of their apartments for almost a year, and it was during that time that I met my lover, Andy Kruzich. Eventually, we moved in together. Andy, like me, is HIV positive. My best friend, Hector Gonzalez, introduced us.

I was working on Fire Island as a houseman for a seventy-year-old lady. This woman became a good friend and was there for me during a tough time when Hector was admitted to the hospital. I went to see him every day I could. Hector, whom I loved so much, was dying. One day, when I went to visit him, the nurse told me he had just died and was no longer in his room. I was in a state of shock. The lady I worked for was a volunteer at the hospital and lived nearby. I went over to her house and broke down."

I don't think that people who are straight realize that when gays lose lovers or significant others, it's the same as when they lose their wives or husbands. They don't realize that gays can have deep love and have the same feeling of actual devotion. Leonce philosophizes about the nature of things in a world tainted by AIDS. "It seems unfair to have lost so many friends at this young age. And it's such a lonely existence. Of course, I have Andy, and I love him very much. But I miss my friends who have died, and I am scared to make new friends if they have AIDS."

"I have a friend I met three years ago who has just come out of the closet. He was a Christian Brother working with the dying in hospitals. That is how he got involved in the AIDS crisis. Now, he does an AIDS program in New Jersey. He is so positive and is doing such wonderful things. He feels he is doing the work that Jesus wants him to do. He is pulling many of us through. He will show up at the hospital, love you, and be there when you need him most."

I wrote earlier about how Leonce was determined to become clean before he died, to find a relationship, to become an actor, to come out publicly to make a difference, to fight the stigmatization, and to educate kids about the epidemic and how to be safe.

Leonce accomplished all of this and much more. He did become clean. He did find a relationship with Andy Kruzich, and they moved to Washington, DC, where he died. And he came out publicly and did incredible work with the AIDS Resource Center in New York. He became the actor he had always wanted to be with the AIDS Theater Project. They put on a gripping play about discovering you had AIDS and brought it to schools throughout the New York area, and then at the end of the play, they would sit on the stage and just field questions from the students about the disease and how to be safe. It had a significant impact. He was always out front in marches, parades, and causes, fighting stigmatization.

Leonce died September 8, 1993.

Leonce did not just follow the steps in the 12-step program; he conscientiously took each step and worked on it, making amends along the way.

He wrote a beautiful card to me in August.

> *Bill, thank you so much for everything you have done for me. Someday, I will pay you back all the money I owe you.* (and he did.) *I really enjoyed Kirkridge, horseback riding, the clear, fresh air, etc. I have the best "buddy" God could have sent me. I love you with all my heart. I now have 18 days clean with NA, and I continue to count each day as a blessing.*
> *Sent with love, Leonce*
> *Thank you for just being you — my very special best friend*

Once he went to Bailey House, our paths only crossed occasionally, except when he came on the Chrysalis retreats. But we would meet now and again, and he would tell me what he was up to. One Thanksgiving before he went to Washington, he stayed over at Edmund House in Perth Amboy and insisted on cooking a

Thanksgiving meal for Andy and me. It was the last time I was to see him.

After the memorial service at Bailey House, Andy Kruzich wrote:

> *Dear Bill,*
>
> *I want to thank you for all your help with Leonce's Celebration of Life. It was very special having you preside over the service; it couldn't have been any other way. I am sure you know how very important you were to Leonce and the change in his life that let him give back so much to all of us. He held a very special place in his heart for you and often shared with me his fondness for you and his thankfulness for coming into his life and making it so much better.*
>
> *I know it must have been as difficult for you as it was for me to lead the service. You did an especially wonderful job; I know Leonce would be pleased. Many people commented on the wonderful service, and you had much to do with it. In your ministry, you must feel good about positively impacting many lives. In this particular instance, your impact was enormous, and I am one of many people who benefited.*
>
> *This Thanksgiving, I remembered, in particular, last year's Thanksgiving when the three of us were together. It is a wonderful memory to have. You were always there for Leonce through the ups and downs, and I have that to be thankful for, as well as beautiful Leonce himself.*
>
> > *Thanks again, Love,*
> > *Andy*

15

Leaving the Office of Pastoral Care

There was just silence; I no longer existed.

I n June 1993, a significant change was made within the inner workings of the diocese. Until now, I had been reporting directly to Fr. Joe Szulwach, who reported directly to the Bishop. Now there would be a change. The Office of Pastoral Care and Social Ministries would become part of Catholic Charities, and we would report to the Director of Catholic Charities, a Sister. The Director of Social Ministries and I dutifully began to meet with the Director weekly during June to get to know each other. Things went pleasantly, with a cup of tea and chatting, until it became official on July 1. Then all hell broke loose.

The Director of Social Ministries was removed as director and put in charge of a second-hand thrift shop in the western part of the diocese, and a new person was appointed Director of Social Ministries. We could not believe it was happening. This man had left a high position in Verizon to work for peace and social justice issues for the Diocese of Metuchen. And now he was humiliated in this way. There were also changes made to our offices. I no longer had a personal secretary and was asked to keep a minute-to-minute log of what I did during the day. The new director also wanted the Chrysalis Ministry's records and financial report. At that point, I told her that it was hands-off and I would leave immediately if she pursued that. I was in the middle of making that a non-profit organization.

So it was not a good beginning, and it went downhill from there. The AIDS priest council supported the re-formation and was not sympathetic to my issues. So, I knew it was over, and I would not waste my energy on nitty-gritty power struggles while I was working with people dealing with life-and-death issues. I let it play out.

One morning, I was told to come to Sacred Heart parish and meet with the same priest who had previously supported our work. Catholic Charities was under his portfolio now. I can't explain the feeling that came over me when I entered his office. I would know exactly how it felt if I ever had to go before a church inquisition. Sitting behind his desk in full priestly garb, he began to fire questions at me, one after the other. The bottom line was I would no longer be Director of Pastoral Care. The working relationship between the Sister and me was not working, and I had to go. That was the first time that such an occasion had happened to me. So I was learning all sides of life.

An interesting side story was that my good friend, Joan deVelder, who had been working with me with the support group we ran at the Church, was upset with this decision, and she made an appointment to meet with the priest the following evening at 6 pm. She came to the appointment, which was not in a good neighborhood, and waited, standing in the dark on the front porch. He never showed up and never answered any follow-up calls. Just the silence, making it as if someone did not exist.

I had experienced that silence earlier. There was silence after the first couple of months of working under the re-organization and several encounters with the director. I no longer existed. There were no phone calls, meetings, exchanges, or communications—just nothing, as if I or the office did not exist. That is a powerful tool the institutional Church uses and is very effective. Then, the call to come to the office.

It is interesting how things started to happen almost immediately. In December, after the call into the office, I needed to do an exit interview with the diocese's chancellor, and then finally, I met with the Bishop. I was asked to write a resignation letter, which I did on December 11, 1993. Of course, it was sad, and some negative feelings crept back in.

So it was over. But I was being taken care of. The bishop said I could continue living at the house the Church had provided me for the time being and could continue my AIDS work in the diocese, but I would not receive any stipend. So, it gave me the needed space, and I was not immediately thrown into the streets.

I was there for another two and a half years before the new pastor wanted to use the house for a deacon from the Dominican Republic who had a family and would work in the parish. I don't exactly remember the details, but I must have written the bishop, explained the work I was continuing to do in the diocese, and inquired about another possible open residence. He was a very gentle man, and you can see that in all his responses:

June 7, 1996

Dear Brother Bill,

Many thanks for your gracious letter bringing me up to date with the activities that you have been carrying out on behalf of people infected with HIV/AIDS. I am very grateful for your continuing ministry in the diocese, and I am convinced that you are touching a great many people in desperate need of the Church's ministry. Your care for these people is surely an example for all of us.

I am deeply sorry I have no solution for you at this time for your housing problem. I know that Father Scott truly needs the house for a deacon who is deeply involved in Hispanic Ministry in that parish and will be helpful in our overall programs reaching out to our Hispanic people. I regret the fact that this presents you with a very serious problem. Even more, I regret the fact that I have no solution for you at this time.

If any possibilities present themselves in the immediate future, I will surely contact you. I would very much like you to continue your ministry in the diocese, but I simply do not have the facilities to offer. I will surely pray that something turns up, so that you can continue to be a blessing for the Church of Metu-chen.

*With prayerful best
wishes,
I am Sincerely in Our Lord,
Most Rev. Edward T. Hughes*

16

The Establishment of Chrysalis Ministry

God enters our lives when
we least expect it.

I had to address how to bring in a salary. I made Chrysalis ministry a non-profit organization with a board of directors made up of the Chrysalis ministry retreat team. Lawyers helped us set this up, and a tax person graciously took care of the annual filings to the IRS almost pro bono. He did that for over ten years. What a blessing this was. What if I had allowed it to be put under the name of the diocese of Metuchen—chills go up and down my spine just thinking about that.

I was president and did not receive a salary for that position, although the board gave me a stipend for the work I had already done while trying to figure out how to support myself. I was always so grateful to them for that.

Over the years, I connected with several AIDS coalitions, which were made up of organizations and interested people gathered together in each county to determine the needs of the AIDS community. They would then decide what organizations within the county could best serve those needs. The federal government would then directly fund these chosen services from the Ryan White Funds.

I started small, and in the first year, I proposed that I be supported to offer pastoral visits to people with AIDS. And it was accepted. This was the first time that any coalition in the state had asked for this. I would need a referral from somebody to do the initial visit, such as a social worker or nurse, and then I would visit that client in their home or at the hospital. I would keep track of my mileage and the time I spent with the person and be reimbursed. So it was a start. I slowly got increasing numbers of referrals and was able to support myself in this way. The federal government was supporting me—how about that!

I mentioned before that I had gone to school to become a massage therapist and a Reiki practitioner. So the following year, I proposed offering massage or Reiki to any client who wished it. With these proposals, I had to go to a board and justify and respond to questions, as they had to choose from the many proposals made that would be most beneficial for the clients. The massage and Reiki proposals were approved. Again, it was the first time in the state that such services were supported. (As you would expect, other counties in different parts of the state heard about this and made similar proposals in their counties). Again, I received referrals. So when I went into a home, it could be for a pastoral, massage, or Reiki visit. Quite awesome.

Then I got enough courage to push for a reimbursement for a four-day Chrysalis ministry retreat that a person might choose to go on. By then, our retreats were becoming very well known and continued to be the only retreat on that scale offered in the state. Again, that was accepted, but only a limited number of spots would be available for any one county. But every little bit helped.

It was a slow process and involved a lot of paperwork, but it enabled me to be supported through my work with Chrysalis ministry. Again, it was because of the tireless work of people like Pat Buckley and so many others who were willing to do the tedious paperwork and deal with government protocol and idiocy that these services were able to reach and make a difference in people's lives.

When I received notice in 1996 that I had to move out of Perth Amboy, I was forced to look elsewhere for a place to live. This time, I was looking for a place for myself; I could no longer expect someone to give me a house. I used to visit all the coalitions in each county to inform them of the services of Chrysalis ministry. I would go to Middlesex, Monmouth, Ocean, and Somerset Counties, which covered a good bit of central New Jersey and the Jersey shore. A nurse in Ocean County, Sharon Owens, told me about a small apartment she used to live in before she bought a house, which she noticed was available, and gave me the information to do a follow-up. Wow! How great was that? And that is when I moved into a tiny apartment in Wanamassa, NJ, on the Jersey shore. The landlady lived in the house and rented this apartment, which had its own entrance with an added benefit: it was on a lake!

In addition, when I moved down to the area, I met Fr. Bob, who was also doing AIDS work and had a center in Asbury Park. He told me about a priest, Fr. Clarke, a close friend at St. Leo the Great Parish in Lincroft, who might have some office space for me. I contacted him and was offered a room out of which I could do my ministry for no cost as long as I wanted. What a generous gift, as we were running on a sparse budget. At times, we collaborated. I did not hesitate to call on him when I was visiting someone dying of AIDS and seeking the sacraments of the church.

I had made a decision not to do a lot of public fund-raising. But we did need money to run the retreats. I remembered what Lou Tesconi had done for Damien Ministries in Washington, DC. I found an updated directory of all the priests in each diocese in New Jersey. For each retreat, I targeted a couple of dioceses and would write a personal letter to each priest and request a donation to help us make the retreat possible for a person living with AIDS. I would write and sign the letter and ask the retreat team to take a group of letters, seal, and post them. And it worked.

This was so clever, and I admire Lou for figuring it out. This way, you did not have to ask the Bishop's permission to raise money in his diocese, which is an extremely sensitive issue. You are making a personal appeal to an individual priest for his own personal donation. Now, that priest can deal with that in any way he wishes. He could take it out of his own pocket, (which many did), from a discretionary fund, or funds set aside for that purpose. And no one needs to know.

That funded our retreats for over ten years. We never hit them up more than once a year, and we could give them statistics on how many attended and direct feedback from those attending on the impact it had on their lives.

17

Experiences of Freedom

*There is no hierarchy of
ministries but only a variety
of gifts.*

T he first national gathering of people working in
HIV/AIDS ministry occurred at Notre Dame
University in 1988. In response to this gathering,
the National Catholic AIDS Network was founded in
1989 by a group of diverse leaders in the Catholic
Church, including clergy and laypeople. NCAN was the
only organization devoted exclusively to helping the
Catholic Church respond with compassion and understanding to the HIV/AIDS crisis. The organization
concentrated on helping Catholic agencies, communities, and individuals by providing educational resources, including conferences, videos, posters, lectures,
and pamphlets, and hosting an annual conference.

It was a very freeing experience for me to attend
these annual conferences and meet people from all over
the country and the international community who were
jumping into the ministry with little knowledge but an
incredible amount of compassion and a deep desire to
learn how to make a difference for the community they
were serving. We were all learning from each other.

As mentioned earlier, it was where I first heard John McNeill speak. I also met a remarkable nun, Sister Jeannine Grammick. Nicholas Kristof wrote about her many years later in his column in *The New York Times*:

> Sister Jeannine Grammick, while working on her doctorate in mathematics, met a gay man who asked for religious help. She organized a liturgical home service for him, which grew into a regular liturgy for gay Catholics in private homes. In 1977, she helped found the New Ways Ministry to support gay and lesbian Catholics. The Vatican tried to suppress her. Her order, the Loretto Sisters, was instructed at least nine times to dismiss her. It passively resisted. Sr. Jeannine would say, "The Vatican tried to suppress me, and it just didn't work."
>
> At a time when much of Christianity denounced gays and lesbians, Sister Jeannine was a beacon of compassion and struggled to educate the Church she loved. She would say, "People always emphasize sex, sex, sex, and it isn't about sex. It is about love. It is who you fall in love with that makes you lesbian and gay. Love is the important thing here, not sex."

New Ways Ministry would always have a table at the annual conferences, and it was there that I met Sr. Jeannine early in my AIDS work. She not only helped me with personal issues but also helped me get involved with the outreach she was doing. She asked me to work with others to arrange conferences in the New

York/New Jersey area to reach out to any groups who would like to explore these issues more deeply. And I did that. I remember one conference we worked on was to invite priests and religious to come together to talk about celibacy and sexuality. This was unheard of; how could you do that? I asked Iona College to allow it to be held on their grounds, and we got a wonderful nun from Seattle, Washington, who had courageously written many well-received books on sexuality, to be our main speaker. We were getting a good response and people were registering.

Brother Jim Liguori was president of Iona College at the time, and he sent me a copy of a letter he had gotten from Cardinal O'Connor indicating that their phones had been lit up by negative calls about the conference. To his credit, Brother Jim let us go through with the day. It was a great success, and all those who attended appreciated it.

After the event, I wrote the Cardinal:

March 5, 1995

I am a member of the Committee that worked on bringing Sr. Fran Ferder to the New York area to speak to interested priests and religious on integrating our sexuality and spirituality. On the eve of the event, it was very disturbing to me to receive a call from the president of Iona College, Brother James Liguori, informing us that your office had been bombarded with calls concerning this conference.

One might have hoped that people would rejoice that so many priests and religious were planning to take the time to dialogue on such an important and significant issue in their lives—especially in contrast to all the negative publicity given in this area in the secular press these days.

I am writing to assure you that Sr. Fran Ferder gave excellent presentations which were fruitful to all those attending and led us in excellent dialogue sessions. She has a deep love for her God and Church. She shared with us her truth, her questions, her insights, and her experiences as a way to challenge us to continue our ongoing integration of our sexuality and spirituality as celibate people. It was an enriching day for all of us, and my only regret is that more people did not take advantage of this opportunity to hear from someone who is so authentic and committed and who is such a wonderful gift to our Church.

Thank you for giving your attention to this letter. Let us pray for each other.

I was experiencing freedom within me at this particular time of my life, which I had never experienced before. The year before the event, we had our province assembly preparing for the 1995 Congregational Chapter. Different formats were used during the assembly to gather brothers to discuss issues. One morning, we were to break up into groups to discuss topics of mutual interest. I spoke to a couple of brothers whom I knew were gay, and I shared with them that I was going to make a late post for a meeting of gay brothers to come together to talk about ways we could support each other. We would meet in a room which was a bit off the beaten path, to make it more comfortable for brothers who may want to attend.

I did post it very conspicuously, but only the two brothers I spoke to earlier were in attendance. So we had our meeting and had a great discussion, and I wanted to share it with the assembled brothers—just to read ten brief statements. As the brothers were regathering after the allotted time, I asked the facilitator for two minutes to do that. But by then, he knew what my group was about and said there would not be time to do it, as they were on a tight schedule. He then gave the assembly a half-hour break.

I was not happy with that, so I went into a separate room during the break and got a large sheet of poster paper and, in large print, wrote the name of our group and the ten statements we had come up with and signed my name at the bottom and went back into the Assembly Hall and pasted it on the wall for all to see. And that is how I came out as a gay man to the brothers. But it was interesting that no brother ever said anything to me about it during or after the assembly.

I knew the statements from these small groups would be circulated to the communities after the assembly, and I wrote a note requesting that the newsprint I had posted on the wall be included:

July 10, 1994
I have enclosed the community survey from the assembly and the newsprint from the meeting with the gay brothers.

Raising the gay issue was not easy for me. It was something I could not not do. I'm sharing my story recently published in a Communications Ministry Inc. newsletter. This organization helps gay and lesbian clergy and religious people deal with the reality of their orientation in their everyday lives. This will give you an idea of where I am coming from.

I received so many mixed signals from you that I felt you were mediating between my wishes and the resistance from the steering committee. Although some of me wanted to do otherwise, I chose to work within the assembly's structure.

There are many myths about homosexuality. The religious right and other conservative groups have infected our society with hate and fear. Our gay brothers must live with this every day in our society, church, and communities. There is a lot of pain and misunderstanding. It is unjust not to address it and allow dialogue.

Please allow our written newsprint to be shared with the brothers and not be prevailed upon by fearful voices. I dream that we can have a support group of gay Christian Brothers within our province so that we can address the issues that concern us and find strength from each other in living our commitment.

Many other congregations have done this, and it has helped many men. There is no other agenda here. Would we rather men remain living in the closet in fear or act out in ways that are harmful to them and our congregation?

Thank you for your understanding and support.

It was included in the statements, which, along with the other groups, were published at the end of the Assembly.

The whole time at the assembly was a very powerful experience for me. Brother Michael Garvey, the congregational leader, was there for the assembly, and he became my hero when, in his opening talk, he said:

As you emphasize the importance and significance of the ministry of teaching, I would love to be able to explore with you further a statement of our last General Chapter in its document of evangelization when it says:

> *There is a need to recognize that within the mission of the Congregation, there is a variety of ministries. Within this variety, there is no hierarchy of ministries but only a variety of gifts. It needs to be emphasized that all of our ministries, approved by the appropriate Superior, contribute to our mission of evangelization.*

18

Creating a Chrysalis

*I now am God's gay little
boy with a so called illness
that he wants me to die
with.*

Our retreat team met after Damien Ministries
assisted us in running our first retreat. We were
searching for a name to call our non-profit
organization. Sr. Mary McGrath suggested the name
"Chrysalis Ministry." How inspired, and what a perfect
name. For it was what we wanted to be about.
We wanted to create a safe space for people to come
together and support each other, get in touch with their
spiritual resources, and allow their lives to be transformed.

We created our mission statement:

> *Chrysalis Ministry exists to create a welcoming and
> safe space for people living with HIV/AIDS to come
> together for mutual support. To create an atmosphere
> where the body, mind, and spirit can be refreshed and
> where hope, joy, and love permeate those places where
> fear, pain, and loneliness prevail.*

A chrysalis is a protective covering for a stage of growth in which the larvae of the butterfly undergo internal changes while quietly and tranquilly at rest before emerging as the beautiful butterfly. Chrysalis Ministry offers that protective place where people can find hope in a time of crisis and emerge into the light and love of the mystery we call God.

In this environment, many activities are offered to get in touch with and strengthen the spiritual resources within themselves. The staff, being conscious of the variety of religious backgrounds of people attending the retreat, make every effort to be respectful of these traditions without alienating those who may not be connected to a particular denomination or belief.

Chrysalis aims to help people clarify their inner source of strength for themselves. During this process, the staff is aware of the need not to proselytize but to support people wherever they might find themselves on this inner journey. In such an atmosphere, the love and acceptance of oneself and others are encouraged to develop a greater sense of community and fellowship.

An extraordinary group of people created this space. Over 40 people at different times volunteered their services over the ten years to run twenty four-day retreat programs and eight-weekend retreats for over 600 people (many who came several times). One hundred fifty men and women, or 25% of those who attended our retreats, died by the end of those ten years that we were made aware of. The retreat team promised those attending these retreats to celebrate the memory of any retreatant who died. We did this in two ways. One way was to read the names of all those who died during a ritual on the third evening of the retreats. The second way to commemorate them was by making a butterfly with their name and placing it on our quilt. The quilt would be rolled out during the healing service, and the names of those newly added would be acknowledged during a powerful healing ritual.

None of this would have been possible without the tremendous support of the many priests of the dioceses of Newark, Paterson, Trenton, and Metuchen who gave generously from their hearts time and again over the years and for the tireless efforts of the staff who worked 15 or more hours on the retreat days making themselves available to those who came. In addition, they put in countless hours at both preparation and evaluation meetings—all on a volunteer basis.

At the end of their retreat experience, we always asked those attending to write down their experience of the retreat. These comments speak for themselves and are what kept us going, for we knew we were making a difference:

> *I had the intention to come on this retreat, get as close as I could to my higher power, and then take my life. The retreat filled up my cup and saved my life.*
>
> ***
>
> *I could not dream there could be so much love in one place—people care. I feel loved and pampered. This was Holy Ground. I never felt so much love.*

***

Once I got the virus, I stopped my life. I felt I had no future. Life was over. I was alone. Since I have been here, I know I am no longer alone. I don't have to crawl into a hole and die. This has made me alive again.

***

God has moved amongst us. I felt His touch.

***

It's a gasoline station. You come and fill up with unconditional love. So much support! Time to get away from what sometimes can be a cruel world. Here I have received from strangers what I have never gotten from my own. It hurts to leave.

***

It is so good to know that there is a place where one can go and feel anxious but safe, sad, and yet happy, and be alone without being lonely.

***

I was able to bring up issues that were buried for years.

***

The staff are great. I'm here because you know my pain and want to ease it. I thank you all.

***

The genuine caring shown for each other. The ability to speak honestly and openly about personal issues without judgment. The chance to share with a cross-section of humanity, positive, negative, black, white, male, female, young, old, married, partnered without prejudice.

***

Chrysalis has been a loving, nurturing, and safe place filled with overwhelming love that taught me I AM SPECIAL and worthy to be loved.

***

It was so restful that I felt a deep sense of security and no longer felt alone.

***

For the first time, I came in contact with my Higher Power. There was acceptance from everyone—black and white. I had fun without booze and drugs. I never thought I would have so many gay friends.

***

It was a once-in-a-lifetime experience and a healing one for me. Now I know that I am not alone, nor will I ever be

***

I loved the atmosphere, the commitment, and the serenity. It gave us a chance to come together without anyone pushing their beliefs on us.

***

The hibernation period of Chrysalis is now over, and we are now beautiful butterflies. We will take the lessons, knowledge, courage, and serenity found in these retreats and go on with our lives, sharing that strength and hope with others.

And there were individual testimonies that people took the time to share with us in letters after the retreat. This one is a letter from a group of musicians who played at one of our retreats:

2/23/93

Dear Bill, Carol, Cheryl, David, Donna, Jean, Joe, Mary Ann, Nancy, and Ty,

Thank you for allowing us the great honor and privilege of participating in this past retreat. We came not knowing what to expect. We certainly did not expect to be accepted, loved, and included in the community that your hard work was able to form on this retreat.

We have the utmost respect for what you are doing through your ministry. We are humbled by it and want you to know how much we admire each and every one of you. Our short time with you has changed our lives and given our work as musicians purpose and direction.

If we can ever be of service to you again in any capacity, please don't hesitate to call. We would be happy to donate our time and energies to bring some peace and happiness to our beautiful brothers and sisters suffering from this terrible disease.

With deep respect and much affection. Tom, Krissi, Bob

Fr. Bill, a priest with AIDS who lived in the Midwest, wrote and asked me to come on our retreat. He was a wonderful soul who touched all of us deeply. He just wanted to be one of the retreatants without any special attention. And he found a safe environment. At one point, a small group asked him to offer Mass with them, which he did graciously and beautifully. When he left to go home, he left me this note:

10/30/98

> *Brother Bill,*
>
> *You are a brother in more ways than one. Thanks for making room for me this weekend. I've come a long way, and a lot of it was just because you all were open and willing to help.*
>
> *I think I even shed priesthood if it was a barrier or mask. I now am God's gay little boy with a so-called illness that He wants me to die with.*
>
> *Keep up the good work.*
>
>
>
> *Lots of love and prayer,*
> *Lots of love,*
> *Bill*
>
>

A couple of months later, a priest from his diocese wrote me a letter:

> *Dear Brother Bill,*
>
> *Fr. Bill, who attended the Chrysalis Ministry retreat in April, died in May. I am enclosing his obituary notice and an article from the* Advocate *that best explains his early death. The immediate cause was a heart attack, likely secondary to Addison's disease. He had discomfort after eating from time to time, and except for the chronic fatigue, he had no real pain, thank God! It was somewhat sudden for us who loved Bill, but we all were thankful not merely for his life and its richness for us but for being spared dementia*

and the slow lingering debilitation so common in AIDS. He died during his first hospitalization.

Bill had attended a wedding in his family on Saturday and, in effect, said goodbye to all his blood family. He was worn out on Sunday. He was staying with his sister, Maureen. At about 3:30 am on Monday (Memorial Day), she caught him as he had a heart attack while in the bathroom. After being stabilized by the rescue squad, he was transported to the hospital.

That afternoon, beginning about 5:30 PM, once each of us, his priest friends, got his room phone number, we each talked to him for 20 minutes to a half hour quite by accident, each of us in effect being able to say "Goodbye" though we didn't realize it at the moment. After talking to his latest and possibly dearest friend, Bob, from 7:30 to 8 pm, he fell asleep, and his heart stopped at 8:10 pm.

Bill often spoke of the gifts that you and your staff shared with him at the retreat. In the name of his family and his closest priest friends, we thank you and your staff for preparing him to give himself back to the loving God who shared him with us for 48 years of life, 22 years of priesthood, and 11 years of sobriety.

I was the one who brought him to Convent Station and was very impressed with the wonderful spirit and graciousness of the entire staff. Please share this note with them and chalk up one great big success for yourselves in what is certainly the most difficult ministry. As I do not feel that his family would be able to respond to your team, I am returning the address list that you sent Bill in the middle of May so you may be assured that it has been kept most confidential. I *found it in his Franklin planner and thought it should be returned to you.*

Fr. David

I responded to his thoughtful letter:

Dear David,

On behalf of the Chrysalis Ministry team, I really want to thank you for your letter and express our deepest sympathy for the passing of a wonderful human being. We so much appreciated your time communicating with us and sharing the details surrounding his death. His loving God did take care of him, didn't He?

Father Bill was a wonderful witness to all of us during the retreat. He desperately wanted just to be Bill and share in the experience. However, at one point, he was asked to celebrate the Eucharist; he willingly did so for those who could attend. It was a very moving experience and one they will always cherish.

At the end of the retreat, Bill left me the following note: (shared above)

It was a wonderful gift to have Bill with us, and thanks for all the encouragement and assistance you gave him to make it possible. We have all been blessed and are now confident that he is in a place where he will be able to assist us in our ministry.

May God bless you in all you do.

19

The Closing of Chrysalis Ministry

The focus of Chrysalis has always been the creation of a safe space where people can truly be accepted for who they are and for wherever they are on their journey.

As I approached the age of 68 and my 50th anniversary as a brother, I decided to close Chrysalis Ministry. We let everyone know a year before we closed that the next three retreats would be our last—two at Xavier Center and our last one at the Carmel Retreat House in Mahwah, NJ. Like Xavier Center, Carmel Retreat House opened its doors to us during the last eight years of Chrysalis for weekend retreats. At these retreats, we invited couples—both gay and straight, both infected with the virus or only one partner infected. Our anxiety about how they would interact with each other was quickly dispelled, and they let us know the incredible need that was met as very intimate issues were placed on the table for open discussion. Interestingly, this is the same Carmelite order that Lou Tesconi had entered from Texas when he went to their novitiate in Washington, DC. I always liked to think he made this happen for us.

Months before the final retreat, I needed to enter the hospital for open heart surgery. Sometimes, people thought that was why I closed Chrysalis Ministry, but that was not true. I had made that decision earlier. I guess my body was telling me it was something I needed to do, but I wasn't too good at listening.

I tried to see if someone wanted to continue with it, but that was not to be the case. The year before we closed, I wrote to all the people who had supported us to inform them of our decision. I would just like to mention some of the great people and real heroes who worked in the early days of this AIDS crisis when it was not the thing to do.

I wrote Pat Buckley from the Visiting Nurse Association, who led the Middlesex AIDS Coalition and took it upon herself to coordinate the activities of the county with both the federal and state governments to bring Ryan White monies to those groups serving the needs of the AIDS population.

> *Dear Pat,*
> *. . . We have been very fortunate to have someone like yourself in the leadership position. We are not aware of half the things that you do for us. You have always gone out of your way to assist and encourage me in every way possible. I am sure our pastoral, retreat, and massage programs were accepted at the state level only through your advocacy. Thank you for that and your willingness to do all the necessary distasteful*

things to build a bridge for us at the state and federal levels.

I wrote Herb Lippman from Lippman, Selznick & Witkowski, who generously assisted us at minimal charge in setting up our non-profit organization and then, for ten years, took care of our annual financial report to the Federal Government.

> *Dear Mr. Lippman,*
> *Thank you again for your generous services to Chrysalis Ministry. We are celebrating our tenth anniversary as a nonprofit body this June, and we consider you one of our longest supporters. It doesn't seem that long ago that you took the time to visit me and discuss how you would help us, and you have been very faithful to your promise.*

I informed Bishop Theodore McCarrick of our closing as he was a generous supporter of our retreats, and he wrote back to me:

> *Dear Brother Bill,*
> *I want to acknowledge your letter of April 1st concerning the retreats given by Chrysalis Ministry.*
> *I appreciate the important work you have been doing, and I am happy to sponsor a retreatant. I am sending you a check for $175 to cover the cost of a retreat for one individual.*
> *I am sorry that you will not continue your work after March 2001. It is so important that we do the*

*best we can to help the people suffering from
HIV/AIDS. May the Lord bless all those whose work
has gone into the ministry in which you give your
time so generously.*

With every good wish, I am

And so, we had our last retreat and said our goodbyes.

We had one thing left to do, and that was to take care
of our AIDS quilt. In those days, AIDS was a death
sentence, and many who came to our retreats knew they
would not be able to make another retreat. Therefore, it
was essential for us and them to create a quilt to remember those who had attended our retreats and died.
We promised them this. Carol O'Neill, our nurse, took
this upon herself as an act of love and kept the quilt
updated, placing their name on a butterfly and sewing
it onto the quilt.

Chrysalis Ministry closed in 2001, and Xavier Center
generously offered to hang the quilt panel on its wall as
a remembrance. For ten years, it was there. In June 2011,
Xavier Center closed its doors as a retreat center, and
we decided to send our quilt panel to the Names Project
Foundation in San Francisco. It became part of the
National Quilt, with 50,000 panels listing 110,00 names.
Wikipedia tells us:

> The NAMES project AIDS Memorial Quilt, often
> abbreviated to AIDS Memorial Quilt or AIDS
> Quilt, is a memorial to celebrate the lives of people
> who had died of AIDS-related causes. Weighing
> an estimated 54 tons, it is the world's largest piece
> of community folk art as of 2020. It was conceived

in 1985, during the early years of the AIDS pandemic, when social stigma prevented many people living with AIDS from receiving funerals. It has been displayed on the Mall in Washington, D.C., several times. In 2020, it returned to the AIDS Memorial in San Francisco and can be seen virtually.

Chrysalis Ministry touched the lives of many who needed a safe environment to share their stories, feel less alone, make new friends, and find new hope. So we remember the 175 names on the quilt and all those retreatants who have died since 2001 and whose names are written in our hearts.

In closing this chapter, I would like to list those on the team who made Chrysalis Ministry possible over this ten-year period.

Team Members
Carol Bachonski, RN Carol Bamesberger, Sr. Helen Bearisto, RC Nancy Begin, RN Cheryl Bryant, Mary Capron, Fr. Damien Charbonneau, Br. Tom Cunningham, CSC Carolyn DeAngelis, David DeNoble, Laura Kelly, Gary Elam, Sr. Eileen Flaherty, OSU, John Frederick, Fr. Angelo Gambatese, Tonya Gilmore, Rev. James Lloyd, Ty Martin, Br. Joseph McAlister, Sr. Mary McGrath, Michael Nelson, RN, Carol O'Neil, Jean Potter, Donna Ritz

Presenters
John Calvi, Fr. Nick Christiani, Joan deVelder, Sr.
Carol Heller, Rev. Bruce Jennifer, Amy Kelinger,
Michael Medick, Edmund Nixon, Jane Selinski

Nurses
Joe Conrad, Howard Barkosky, Adrian Gil, Mary
McAndrew, John McCausland

Storytellers
Stephanie Stoy, Bob Stoy

A Personal Reflection

In my mind, the focus for the Chrysalis retreats was to
create a welcoming, safe space where people could truly
be themselves and be free to explore the sustaining
spiritual resources within so that when they left the
retreat experience, they would not find themselves
alone.

I felt very uncomfortable with religious language.
Many use it to hide from dealing with the real mysteries
of life. But it is essential to support a person wherever
they are because when they leave us, that is what they
take with them. We aim to help people clarify who God
is for them without feeling they need to embrace any
particular belief.

As a gay man, I have had a love/hate relationship
with my church. It was pathological for me to believe
their statements about myself. For my mental health, I
needed to separate myself physically and emotionally
from that abuse. So, I find myself very much on the

outside looking in and not wanting any involvement with the institutional church.

I don't have a lot of anger now, although I certainly can react negatively to pronouncements or insensitive statements by church authority figures. But my life is no longer controlled—I do not give them that power anymore. I have more sadness than anger—sadness for what the church could be.

As I wrote earlier in this book, the passage from the Book of Ezekiel touched me profoundly and helped me on my healing journey. It freed me in many ways and made me sensitive to others who feel misunderstood and oppressed by religion. That is why Chrysalis has always focused on creating a safe space where people can be accepted for who they are and wherever they are on their journey.

20

I Discovered I Was Loved

I lived by the Lake
And we sat side by side
I reached out my hand
It fell upon yours
Nothing else mattered
A bond was formed.

I debated within myself for a long time whether to include this chapter in my memoirs. It is very personal, strikes the deepest core of my being, and is about the most significant and all too brief periods in my life. Fears of any intimacy, deeply rooted within me over the years, consistently paralyzed me. I slowly faced them one by one, and these same fears surfaced again as I started this chapter. I decided to write the chapter as honestly as possible and then decide what to do with it. I take this caution because it is more than just about me.

Toward the end of my time with Chrysalis Ministry, I increasingly placed myself in situations that made me vulnerable. And that was not a bad thing.

In a journal note on 6/1/97:

I hide from my God because I fear his disapproval, condemnation, displeasure, not being good enough, and not doing enough. I do not bring myself as I am to my God; I try to present someone else—a person I think He wants to see. How can I relate if I hide who I am from the person I want to relate to? I don't even relate to myself, for I do not accept myself as I am.

I have hid too long. I want to live each moment fully. I want to open up fully to the unknown moment and bring my total self to it. I hide from my brothers because I feel they will not accept me as I am. I always hid from my family, only tried to live up to their expectations, and only did the things that pleased them.

It seemed that after almost five years of therapy with John McNeil, I hadn't gotten much further along, although that was not true. As I was preparing for my last session with John McNeil on 6/11/97, I made a list of things I had learned and a list of future steps.

What have I learned?
- *To accept myself as I am—a gay man*
- *To accept my mother as she is and learn to place boundaries around the relationship*
- *To become more autonomous in my relationship with the Congregation*
- *To be less afraid of relationships in my life*
- *To be less fearful of my God*

Where do I go from here?
- *Know there is a possibility for a relationship*
- *Find a spiritual practice that is meaningful for me*
- *Seek or create a supportive group of people in my life*
- *Learn to be with myself*
- *Confront my death and my fears around it so that I can be fully alive*

After my last session with John McNeil, I wrote down some notes from that encounter:

- *Trust God is with you as you are.*
- *Let go of messages received.*
- *Pray before and after.*
- *Always in a loving, caring, free context.*
- *Be open to daily opportunities to receive the gift of another in your life.*
- *Trust you will not be swallowed up and lose your identity but you can set boundaries. Gayness and a relationship with God are not mutually exclusive—trust this.*
- *Trust that God knows you completely; when you enter His presence, there will be no surprises— Welcome home. Bill, I was always with you.*

Almost a year later, I wrote in my journal on May 28, 1998:

> *Love is the one law you need to obey. Open your ears to hear when old rules and laws need to be broken. (The Gospel of Gabriel).*

Two days later, on May 30, 1998, I wrote:

Thank you, JC, for making this day possible — a day created from all eternity for me. You have made it special. I hear your words clearly: "You are my beloved, in whom I am well pleased." Why would you do this for me? I never never thought it would be possible. To take away my fear. To erase my guilt. Let me see with your eyes! How beautiful, how good, how holy, how sweet. You knew I could only receive your love when I was loved. I just never felt I could genuinely receive it. Thank you for your gift. Please help me cherish and nurture it. And always find you there and know it is your love I am receiving.

Brother John had asked to visit me that weekend in Wanamassa, NJ. He was someone I had lived with in a community thirty-five years previously. Over the years, we had crossed paths briefly but had no real contact after I was sent to the West Indies to teach in 1963. He was a year older than me—a gentle, courageous soul. I knew almost immediately he had come to visit because he loved me. I knew it was mutual, but I could never have had the courage to take that initiative.

I had intimacy issues (have I said that before???). I had never opened my being to another person. I wrote in my journal earlier that summer:

Why can't I receive love? Where is the key that will open the door of my heart? If I open my heart to another person's love, I will be overwhelmed and unable

to fulfill all the expectations of the other. (This is the
key buried deep within, which keeps the door closed.)

How does one write about a period that was so beautiful yet so painful? We lived at a distance from each other, and our paths did not cross often. We worked on scheduling times to meet. These times were scheduled well in advance to take advantage of opportunities to hang out that would work for each of us. Of course, my work with Chrysalis was still all-encompassing, and I kept asking myself if I was using my work to run away from something so precious because of my fears and not give myself permission to enjoy this friendship. Being always available and on the go was such an integral part of my life, and I knew it was an area that needed my focus. It was beginning to affect me physically, but I did not give it the attention it needed.

I put together a timeline because, as you will see, it gets confusing:

5/30 1998: John visited me.

8/2000: John was diagnosed with cancer and began chemotherapy.

10/2000: John ended chemotherapy—it was not effective.

10/12/2000: John had surgery to remove the tumor. John went to St. Joseph's for recovery.

11/2000: I was diagnosed with 80% blockage of an artery and had heart catheterization with a stent.

1/2001: I had emergency open heart surgery—double by-pass. I went to De La Salle nursing home in Lincroft for recovery.

2/2001: John began new "miracle" treatment up through 5/2001. He responded well to it.

4/2001: I had pains in my chest—a kink in the mammary gland used during surgery—heart cauterization—stent placement.

5/2001: John finished the new miracle treatment and responded well. He returned to making pastoral visits at Holy Name Medical Center in Teaneck, NJ.

6/2001: I requested a sabbatical year.

8/2001: John had summer vacation with De La Salle Brothers in South Jersey—I joined him for three days.

9/2001: I celebrated 50th Anniversary as a brother. John attended.

10/2001: I went on a sabbatical, which included taking a train cross country to stay with my sister in Malibu for a rest.

1/2002: John was told the cancer had returned.
2/2002: I went to New Mexico from California for the start of the renewal program.

Within two years after John's visit, in August 2000, he was diagnosed with multiple myeloma cancer along with a stomach tumor and began chemotherapy, which continued into October of that year. But there was no shrinkage of the tumor in the stomach, and he had surgery to remove the tumor on October 12, 2000, and went to St. Joe's for recovery. I did get to visit John there, but around this period, I began to experience some symptoms of tiredness and brief periods of short-ness of breath, both of which were new to me.

In November 2000, I was diagnosed with an 80% blockage in my left anterior descending artery. I had a heart catheterization where a stent was inserted, and the procedure was declared a success. However, when chest pain continued during my cardio rehabilitation, I was sent to the emergency room at the end of January 2001, where it was determined I needed emergency open heart surgery as cell growth from the stent place-ment was blocking the artery again. I had the double bypass surgery the next day. My surgeon, Dr. Brook De Jeune, knew the De La Salle Brothers in Lincroft, NJ, and asked them if I could go to their nursing facility for rehabilitation since I was living alone. I have always been deeply grateful to my surgeon for looking out for me this way and for the brothers who opened their doors to me as they did in Syracuse and helped me get back on my feet.

However, the recovery was not immediate, and I had a lot of fears about going back to my apartment and being alone and trying to put my life back together. When I continued having pain in April of that year, it was determined, after follow-up testing, that a kink had developed in the mammary artery that was used in my bypass surgery. I had to go through another heart catheterization and have a stent inserted there. During all of this, an excellent cardiologist, Dr. Christopher Pierson, came into my life and helped me change my whole outlook on my illness and gave me the confidence to live my life fully once again. Setbacks slowly receded, and I began to address what I wanted to do with my life. I felt I needed to rest and give myself time to get back on my feet, and I decided to request a sabbatical year, which I had never done before. I felt it was the only way to receive money to support myself during this recovery time, pay for my apartment, and discern my next path.

My request was granted, and I began planning things I wanted to do during the sabbatical year. Also, my 50th anniversary was coming up in September 2001. The brothers always had a big celebration for this event, and I sent invitations to all my family and friends to share this day with me. I had never done anything like this before, but I think my skirmish with death helped me make this a celebration of life.

My sister Agnes came in from California. My brother and my older sister, Mary Ann, were there, along with my nephews and great nieces, as well as close friends Joan deVelder and Jean Potter, who had always been so supportive of me, my spiritual director, Kathy Begley, and the Chrysalis ministry team, for which I had a deep gratitude for helping me create such a special place for those with AIDS.

Br. John went back to chemotherapy until January 2001, after his stomach surgery to remove the tumor. Then, in February 2001, he began a new miracle treatment for cancer called stem cell transplant therapy, which continued into May of that year. He responded well to it and returned to live in his religious community. This all took place while I was having my open heart surgery and going through my cardiac rehab and recovery.

Br. John had always loved spending time with the De La Salle Brothers in Ocean, NJ, during his August vacations, and he had been doing that for several years. They loved him there. He was delighted to be able to be there in August 2001, and he invited me to come down and spend a couple of days with him, which I did. It was a delightful couple of days as we both had survived significant health issues, and Br. John was optimistic about his recovery. In the fall, his strength returned to allow him to continue his ministry at Holy Name Medical Center. He spent his time on the oncology floor.

John joined me on my 50th celebration, and I had my picture taken with him that day, which I have always kept close to me. As a side note, I was the only one in the group of brothers celebrating their 50th that day who wore a suit and tie. One of the guests, who I did not know, who was at the celebrations, challenged me as to why I did this. I was initially taken aback; I felt that to be a strange remark to make on this special day. I was surprised. I harbored no anger but felt sad for him—I wished he could be freer.

It was a painful time to go on sabbatical, but I knew it was something I had to do if I was to try to put my life back together. But at the same time, I did not want to be that far from Br. John. I took a train across the country and stayed with my sister in Malibu for a couple of months to rest before going to Santa Fe, New Mexico, for a three-month renewal program from February to

April 2002. This was run by the De La Salle Brothers (once again !)

In January, 2002, Br. John's energy began to decline, and he started to have periods of increased tiredness. He was told the cancer had returned. It was a devastating blow to him, as he had believed in the treatment. Eventually, with the help of his sister, he reached inner peace with everything as it unfolded. I went to New Mexico in early February to start my renewal program, which was part of the sabbatical year. I was only there a couple of days when I called John to tell him about my arrival and find out how he was doing. He told me he had chosen to live with the brothers in the community and in his own bedroom, where he felt most comfortable. The next day, the Director of the Program came to me and told me he had a phone call for me. I learned that John had passed during the night, and the brothers found his body on the floor of his bedroom in the morning.

His sister let it be known that she would like me to give his eulogy. Br. Jack called and told me the province would take care of the plane trip and car rental expenses so I could return. I flew out the next morning and was able to attend the wake and give the eulogy.

My heart was broken, but I was strong for him. I couldn't say publicly that we loved each other. This was my eulogy:

> *John, I am sorry I wasn't here these past few days. You know I wanted to be.*
> *I lived with Brother John for the first time 43 years ago at Power Memorial Academy in Manhattan. Af-*

ter those years, our paths seldom crossed (which is part of our lives as brothers) until John made it a point to renew our friendship on a visit to South Jersey a couple of years ago.

As one gets older, it is nice to have someone to share memories with, to share one's transition to the winter season, to tear away some of the walls one has built up over the years to protect oneself and share meaningful things. If we are lucky, we might find one person in our lives to walk this path with — to find someone as authentic as John is rare.

We sat and looked out over the lake, walked the beach, and, of course, went shopping for all sorts of crazy things for his friends — tie-dye shirts, beads, and the like. But you know this, because you received them.

Two life-giving things for John were his ten summers with the De La Salle Brothers in Ocean City and his 19 summers at Boston College. John would start planning for his trip to Ocean City months in advance. He looked forward to renewing his friendships, getting caught up on the news, and just reading.

But I shouldn't say just reading, should I, John?

He would read these ponderous theological works while meticulously underlining passages and rereading many until he understood.

John, you said your 19 years at Boston College kept you on the cutting edge.

He wanted to bring the best to his students. This is what Br. John was all about — a total dedication of his life to his students. Of course, few students realized the arduous preparation and his strong desire to give them what they needed for their life's journey. But some did, and they expressed their appreciation for his efforts—especially on the occasion of his 50th anniversary as a brother and on his retirement from teaching.

Remarks made by past students last night at the wake typify this:

> *"He was just good to be around."*
> *"He was down to earth."*
> *"He radiated an inner peace."*
> *"He had a wonderful sense of humor.*
> *He greeted me with "Shalom, Baby!!!"*
> *"He is still my teacher; I will never forget him."*

One student left a picture of Dorothy Day in the casket, and on the back, he wrote: "I know how much you loved Dorothy Day. And like Dorothy, to this day, many people quote things you have also said."

Another student, with tears in his eyes, shared, "His death has taught me to connect with people you love before it is too late."

A man is measured by how he handles the most difficult moments of his life.

John, you were tested, and you came up big.

John's decision to retire from teaching was very painful. The circumstances surrounding his decision would have crushed most people. But John turned this to good. He immediately shifted gears and poured all his energies into becoming a pastoral minister at Holy Name Hospital. He used all his skills, knowledge, and experience to touch those facing momentous decisions in their own lives.

A pastoral minister from Holy Name Hospital shared. "Br. John did not meet people; he engaged people. When one does that, wonderful things can and did happen."

Anna knows best the courage it took him to face his own illness and especially the treatments that followed. John often said, "Anna is my strength; she is my Rock of Gibraltar; she is always there for me."

Br. John did everything he could to reverse his illness while accepting God's will for him, although he wanted very much to live. This was exemplified during his only-too-brief period of remission. At that time, he returned to Holy Name Hospital and impacted the lives of those on the oncology floor.

John appreciated the supportive and caring space provided by Brothers Ben and Tom during his illness. He delighted in telling others how they could spend up to two hours having supper at the end of the day. He took particular pride in mentioning how they all worked together in preparing and cleaning up after a meal. This was a special time for him, and it meant a lot.

He has been our teacher to the end. He has taught us much.

Thank you, John, for your kindness, gentle spirit, and selfless generosity, for genuinely being a brother to all you met, and especially for being a brother to me.

I later wrote a poem for myself:

JOHN

You were so free
following your heart
You came back into my life
quite deliberately too
Hi, I'm here
No questions, please

How did I know
You were there for me
No words were needed
I was blown away
After 35 years
Why so long?

They made it wrong.
And we obeyed
Built walls
To hide our pain
Now or Never
Don't run away

I lived by the Lake.
And we sat side by side.
I reached out my hand.
It fell upon yours
Nothing else mattered
A bond was formed

It would never be broken
By either you or me
But we took different paths
As if it wasn't meant to be

First cancer for you
And Open Heart for me

Arriving in Santa Fe
during my sabbatical year
Obeying the rule
Too easy for me
You in Oradell
In a community

I called you that night.
We talked for a while.
You sounded good
No alarms were heard
I hit the sack
Feeling all was well

I was called to the phone.
The next morning, and told.
You were found on the floor.
To be heard from no more
I flew back that day
Not knowing what to say

So many were there.
Speaking highly of you
I was drinking it all in
As a eulogist would do
Yet, could not share what we had
With family and friends

I was proud of what I said
It came from my heart
Spoke of walks on the beach
And the crazy things you bought
They must have known I loved you

But not of my broken heart

You are remembered by many.
Our teacher to the end
Thank you for your kindness,
Gentle spirit, selfless friend
And, of course, being my brother
And being so much more

If I had to live it over
I would never have left your side
We were both on healing paths
Which took us apart
Now my heart is broken
And I've lost all the parts

You gave me a gift
which no one else could
I gave you my heart
and know that I have loved
You have given me yours
May we never be apart.

21

Restarting My Life

*Because of your struggles
you grew in ways that otherwise would not have been
possible.*

This is how my sabbatical year played out:

November 2001: Went to Iowa to complete the Reiki Healing
Hands Program with Kunzang Dechen Chodron.

December 2001: Spent some restful time with my sister in
Malibu, CA.

January 2002: Attended a workshop at the Esalen Institute
In Big Sur, CA with Frank Ostaseski on the End of Life
Counseling program that he had created.

February 2001: Attended a three-month Renewal Program
at the Sangre de Cristo Center run by the De La Salle
Brothers in Sante Fe, New Mexico, which ended on May
14, 2002.

May 2002: Completed my Reiki Jin Kai Do Mastership program with Reiki Master Gilbert Gallego in Virginia.

June 2002: Attended a Mindfulness-Based Stress-Reduction
training with Jon Kabat-Zin at the Omega Center in Rhinebeck, NY.

It gave me the time to complete Reiki programs that I had been drawn to and to explore new possibilities like the End of Life Counseling program. Frank Ostaseski was seeking participants for this program in the upcoming year. I was all ears. Something resonated deeply within me.

After John's death, I returned to Sangre de Cristo in Sante Fe, New Mexico, to continue the renewal program, an essential element of the sabbatical year. Over twenty-five other priests and religious people from all over the world were in attendance. Many had been in leadership positions for years and needed time to relax and renew themselves. The De La Salle Brothers created a healing space and brought in leading teachers of the day to gently update and challenge our thinking. We each had a spiritual director who was a key component for our three months together. I was blessed with Sr. Vincentia, an older sister who lived in Albuquerque and came out regularly to the Center. She was very down-to-earth and skillful. She did not give advice but gently asked questions for you to grapple with. She sensed my hurt and pain and gave me the space I needed to sit with all of this and allow healing to take place.

The daily liturgies and prayer brought me back to where I was twenty years previously. I did not run away but stayed with the process and tried to see with new eyes. Sr. Vincentia gave me an exercise to reframe my life story as a call to life and growth and place it in the context of my relationship with Jesus. It was a challenge for me to do because I had let go of so much of my previous religious practices. But I went along with it and wrote:

> *You called me Jesus at the age of 14. I knew then you wanted me to be a Christian Brother—you were saying, "Follow me." At age 17, I entered the Congregation. I came with my emotional wounds and weaknesses. But you were there with me always. For the next 29 years, you provided an environment I needed to survive as a brother and a wounded human being. You put people in my life at the right moment to save me from myself—indeed, they were my guardian angels. You deeply touched my life through them during my most desperate times. No matter where I was sent, people were there to help me through my most difficult times. You were always in a relationship with me—touching my life through others.*
>
> *Then, you gave me the courage to leave my cocoon—the community. I no longer needed to hide. I no longer needed its protection for my survival. What a grace. For the next 21 years, you led me into my inner self and helped me begin to discover who I was. Again, you placed countless people in my life to hold my hand and be with me on this scary journey. You did not leave me alone, although I was physically alone and felt abandoned often.*
>
> *For these 50 years, you have used my journey to minister to those you put into my life. You and I know what a fragile instrument I was, that you, not me, touched their lives. When I physically collapsed and could do no more, you healed me and made it pos-*

sible for me to renew and strengthen my body, mind, and spirit here at Sangre de Cristo.

Is this no relationship with Jesus? Teach me why I need to diminish what we have. To deny or hide the beautiful things you have done for me. Please heal our relationship and help me never to feel a need to deny it again.

Well, that was pretty awesome. Then, I was asked to have Jesus respond. I wrote:

I was there when you were in your mother's womb. I formed you and was delighted in you. Your parents were wonderful people who always did what they thought best and had to live and struggle with their own wounds.

I was delighted you responded to my call. I could not protect you from your pain and suffering, but you knew I was close by. Because of your struggles, you grew in ways that would otherwise not have been possible. And it was because of this developed sensitivity I could use you to touch the lives of so many.

It was a wonderful day to see you break through your cocoon in mid-life and begin your inner journey. This journey is never easy, and I know how difficult it was for you to accept and proclaim the person you were created to be.

I, too, struggled with religious authorities in my lifetime and paid the price for it. I understand your conflicts with hierarchical structures that often do not open their hearts to issues that deeply affect the lives of many.

Our relationship is important to me. I understand your confusion and pain over the years with Church and congregational issues. It is a turbulent period with major painful transitions taking place. It is important not to let our relationship suffer because of these tensions. As always, I am with you and as deeply in love with you as I was the day you were born.

Wow! Equally as awesome.

At the end of my three months during our closing retreat, I wrote a prayer in the spirit of continuing my new relationship with Jesus:

Jesus, my heart is full of gratitude and has little ink-lings of joy as I end my retreat. Once again, you have made me your special friend.

"Come see where I live and stay a while."

You blessed me with Vincentia, reframed my life story, and allowed me to reconcile myself with you.

When the prodigal son comes home after being away for so long, you open your arms and ask no questions, as if you knew it was a journey that had to be taken.

You have gifted me with the sacred realization that I am an incarnation of your love.

Help me live this fully with joy in all aspects of my daily life.

I desire to deepen my relationship with you and share all parts of my life. By being love, I want to bring the message of your love to all those in my life.

You have brought me to the waters of new life. You have given me another chance at life. Help me never let your hand go again until I am with you forever. Amen.

Quite awesome again. These three months healed me and gave me a new enthusiasm for life and all its possibilities.

22

The Zen Hospice Project

*Invite "death" in for a cup
of tea—sit with it—and let
it talk to you. This is what
the course is all about.*

On my return from my sabbatical, I received permission to apply for admission into the End of Life Counseling Program created by Frank Ostaseski, whom I had met at the Esalen Institute in California. Frank had created and ran a Zen hospice for 17 years and trained over a hundred volunteers to provide 24-hour care to the residents. Frank taught the integration of the spiritual dimensions of living, dying, and transformation. It was a path of service emerging out of Buddhist spirituality.

In Frank's last couple of years as director, he began creating an innovative training program to establish a national network of professionals and volunteers who worked with those facing life-threatening illnesses and the systems that served them.

I was to be part of the second group in this innovative program. My group was made up of 23 medical doctors, nurses, social workers, chaplains, and volunteers from hospitals, hospices, and other healthcare institutions from all over the country. We met in San

Francisco nine times for seven four-day weekends and two ten-day intensive retreats. Between these meetings, we were given assignments and did fieldwork in our local communities.

In January 2003, I went on my first weekend experience. While in San Francisco, I stayed with a community of De La Salle brothers (again!!!), where one of our brothers also resided while doing his doctoral studies.

To give you a sense of the depth of the program, I want to share with you part of Frank's opening remarks to us:

> *You know how to do this already.*
>
> *We become frightened because we have forgotten.*
>
> *We are together to support each other in remembering that the theme this weekend is initiation.*
>
> *There is a voice in the recesses of our mind that tells us, "Someday I will die."*
>
> *We don't want to be too close to this voice, which speaks to us when a loved one dies.*
>
> *How we listen to or turn away from that voice determines how we live our lives.*
>
> *Invite "death" in for a cup of tea—sit with it—and let it talk to us.*
>
> *This is what the course is all about.*
>
> *Initiation is introducing one into a new world.*
>
> *We are beginning a journey with people we don't know and we don't know how it will turn out.*
>
> *It will take us deep into ourselves, and we will question our most basic beliefs.*

Helplessness and insecurity will be our constant companions, breaking our hearts open.
It will take courage and flexibility.
We will find ourselves "caught learning."

The sense of awe and wonder at death breaks the spell of complacency in our lives.
The beginner mind is a willingness to stay open.
We need to be empty—willing to surrender, drop pride and fear, and relinquish what is familiar.
Be open to "Don't know, mind."

There is a greater wisdom beyond acquired knowledge.
It is not about acquiring new skills.
It's about you changing—then the way you do the work changes.
Get back to your true self and let that show up at the bedside.

Yes, I knew this was where I needed to be at this time in my life.

While visiting my sister in Malibu, I did some field work at St. John's Health Center in Santa Monica, CA. One of my most significant early visits was with a man who was a Christian Brother at one time but whom I did not know. I took notes during my fieldwork:

He has melanoma, which has spread to the lungs and brain. The first day, I just sat with him for about an hour. He was not very coherent at times because of some swelling in the brain. I made some phone calls for him, which took time because of his confusion.

Today, when I came into the hospital, he had asked one of the chaplains to leave a message for me to drop by. He was much more alert, and we had a good chat. He could share what was going on and do a life review. He is aware he is having an experimental treatment, which is his last chance. He will be coming in for a second treatment, and if he does not respond to that, there will be no other options. We were able to get to a deeper level than our previous visits.

As I was leaving, I remembered a stone in my pocket that I had picked up at a prayer service that said, "You are precious." I felt it was appropriate to give it to him. I told him to remember he was precious in the eyes of God and the people in his life. He grasped the stone and my hand, shut his eyes, and tearfully thanked me. He shared how he was questioning the meaningfulness of his life and continued to share how he is making a conscious effort to share this diagnosis with everyone he meets. He continues to be amazed at the outpouring of love he receives.

The teachers were in a league of their own: Frank Ostaseski, the founder of the Zen hospice; Angie Stephens, a long-time counselor for people dealing with end-of-life issues; Charles Garfield, founder of the Shanti project, which reached out to people with AIDS; Rachel Naomi Remen, MD, teacher, and author of several books; Frances Vaughn, psychologist and educator; Ram Dass, beloved spiritual teacher; Norman

Fischer, Zen Priest; Rabbi Alan Lew and Angeles Arrien, both well-known authors and speakers in their field.

I will share one more thing here to give you an in-depth look at the work they were challenging us with.

> *Jesus said in the Garden of Gethsemane,*
> *"I am sorrowful unto death; remain with me and watch."*
> *He doesn't say take it away—just be with me.*
> *Everyone keeps falling asleep.*
> *Jesus knows no one can do this but still puts out the request.*
> *To be companions, we travel with the person side by side.*
> *There is no healer and healed.*
> *It is like "Walking through life holding hands."*

> *In Zen practice, the student must have an interview with his teacher.*
> *He needs to be very mindful on entering the room.*
> *The student needs to pay close attention to everything in the moment, so that he will be available to answer the question upon entering the room.*
> *In preparation, the student is aware of turning the doorknob handle, pushing the door open, and sitting on the cushion.*

> *This is the way we need to go into the room of the dying.*
> *And we will be a trustworthy soul.*

The patient just wants you to be with him.
"To be of service" distinguishes between service and helping or fixing.
When we help, we use our own strength. It is a relationship of inequality.
We incur a debt—people feel a need to reciprocate.
When we serve, our whole being serves
Our wounds, our helplessness, and our fears become the meeting place of the other.
It is a relationship of equals.

Help sees the person as weak.
Fixing sees the person as broken.
Service sees the person as a whole.

I had to find a place to do my fieldwork in New Jersey between classes. I contacted the Visiting Nurse Association about volunteering in their hospice program, began a process of training and orientation, and commenced my fieldwork with them.

The depth of the information shared with us and the consistent opportunities for meditation and other practices during our time in San Francisco were at a level I never encountered. I reached a depth I never knew possible, and when I completed the program, I created a meditation practice for myself, which I have been able to build upon.

It was exciting that I noticed a new energy and desire for life when I returned to NJ between the four-day classes. One of these times, I spent six days making significant changes in my apartment and created a space to teach my Reiki classes, to have both a healing circle and a space to offer Reiki to those interested. This new space also included a permanent meditation area where I could go whenever I wished. Finally, I also created a separate workspace that I desperately needed.

I wrote in my journal:

> *I have a new outlook on life. I am no longer a person recovering from a heart condition but somebody who is looking for ways to be there for others. I want to ensure it comes from my meditation and not my need to do it.*

I am sharing some wisdom teachings I absorbed during these nine months. These resonated deeply with me and gave me some confidence in beginning my work with the dying.

> *There is no real service unless both people are being served.*

> *Five primal fears of the dying person are: Fear of the unknown, Fear of abandonment, Fear of body disintegration, Fear of loss of control, and Fear of pain.*

> *There is not a healer and a healed. We travel with each other side by side.*

> *We often are busy wanting a person to be in a particular place, and we miss seeing them where they are.*

> *Discover where you can connect and find a way to get around the obstacles to meet them where they are. Let*

that evolve—it may not look like what we want. Be surprised!!

Just being you is enough.

How to serve the dying: Come into the room, sit down, feel your body and your breath, watch your tendency to make something happen, talk less, listen more, touch when appropriate, and respond to what is actually happening in front of you.

The most healing thing we can do for another person is to be present and give our undivided attention — without judgment or need to fix it.

Death is a process—all we need to do is be there. There is no such thing as a good death or a bad death. It is what it is, and that is okay. It is not up to us to make it happen a certain way.

If you are in contact with your own experience, you will be able to be present to the experience of the other. Trust that.

Everyone has a right to their own spiritual journey. We should never impose our beliefs or values on another. We have not walked in their shoes. There are many spiritual paths. There is no one right way.

These are five precepts created by Frank Ostaseski as guidelines for his volunteers:

1. *Welcome everything; push away nothing.*
2. *Bring your whole self to the experience.*
3. *Don't wait.*
4. *Find a place of rest in the middle of things.*

5. Cultivate, don't know mind.

In our last class, we were given twenty-five 3 x 5 index cards and asked to write a short message to each group member. The idea was that when we returned home, we could draw on these cards as reminders and support for our work in the world. I want to share some of the cards I received, which were overwhelming and life-giving:

> It has been an absolute delight to share this year with you. I have so much respect for you. Your gentle, loving presence, your wit and humor, your great generosity, and your courage in adversity are an inspiration as well as a joy. May you experience all the greatest life has to offer.
>
> ***
>
> Your great steadfastness has been a comfort and an inspiration to me. I will so much miss you. Remember, my dear brother, you are so very loved.
>
> ***
>
> Bill, you are so sweet and so gentle. And so funny! Blessings always.
>
> ***
>
> I have grown so incredibly fond of you this year. I feel like I have witnessed a true transformation. I so appreciate your voice, your insights, and your humor. You are an amazing, courageous man.
>
> ***

A gentle, sweet, quiet heart whose very presence ponders healing for all the hurting healing hearts he encounters

***

You add a whole new meaning to the old adage, "Still waters run deep." I have learned so much from you this year and cannot imagine what it may have been like without your presence and insights. In the small groups, I had the opportunity to experience your compassion and stillness, your capacity to be present with and hold another's pain. That is a gift that I am sure you have cultivated over a lifetime of experience and personal pain. You are masterful in your practice of deep, loving-kindness. Thank you for your humor, generosity (especially your notes), and for holding me so gently in your heart.

***

Bill, remember that dying is falling into love. With deepest appreciation and gratitude for your presence in my life.

***

Your contemplative, compassionate, and loving being has been a constant inspiration to me this year. You also have tremendous humility and a wonderful sense of humor. The special qualities you embody will be of great service as you accompany the dying on their journeys. I wish you an ever-deepening relationship with Mystery. Much love and much joy.

***

May you deeply trust your capacity, by your presence, to bear exquisite witness and to affect possibilities for profound healing. I'm a witness.

***

Your ability "to cut to the chase" in such a quiet, wise, and humorous way has been a constant source of wonder. You have such a big heart and fine intellect. Thank you for your note taking and sharing. Thank you for your listening.

So, I was with people like that. It says it all. Yes, I restarted my life. How can I put into words the deepest gratitude I have for Frank, my teachers, and those I shared the experience with? What a life-changing two years—my sabbatical, followed by this program.

23

My Last Years
of Official Ministry

I am Bill Stevens, who is a
member of the Congregation
of Christian Brothers.

T he next part of my life would be equally exciting
and expanding. Upon completing my end-of-life
counseling program in November 2003, I pursued employment with the VNA Hospice in New Jersey
as a chaplain. I would eventually include Reiki in my
ministry to the nurses, families, and patients. I was 70
years old and would remain in this ministry for ten
years, working three days a week with them.

I also continued my studies in Reiki with incredible
teachers during this period. In addition to Gilbert
Gallego and Kunzang Dechen Chodron, I studied with
an inspiring animal Reiki Teacher in California, Kathleen Prasad, and Frans Stiene, a unique and extraordinary teacher from Australia who transformed how I
taught and practiced Reiki. It is unusual to have something like this happen after 18 years of practice.

The simplest way to explain why this had such an
impact on me, without going into a lot of details, is to
say that Frans spent several years in Japan to research

the beginnings of Reiki, and he discovered the different spiritual Japanese traditions that influenced the Founder of the System of Reiki, Mikao Usui. He found that Mikao Usui taught Reiki as a spiritual practice. He had no standard curriculum, and his teachings were often one-on-one meetings with his students, sharing spiritual practices (meditations) and guiding them on their spiritual journey (practicing the precepts). After learning Buddhist meditation practices from both Frank Ostaseski and Kunzang Dechen Chodron, I was very excited to understand that the core teachings of Reiki were basically about a meditation practice—going deep within ourselves.

It was so freeing for me to begin teaching Reiki not as a structure, ritual, or belief system but as getting in touch with our true self through meditation and offering Reiki from that space. Following the simple precepts that Mikao Usui taught were merely stepping stones to deepening this practice. It helped unite my spiritual life, work, and presence on this planet. It isn't easy to put into words, but transformative best describes it.

In September 2012, I was asked to be one of the main presenters at the Pennsylvania Hotel's New York Reiki Conference. I was asked to speak on "Reiki at the End of Life." Dave Gorczynski and Inoshi Denizen organized the event to bring Reiki to the attention of the healing professions. Frans was one of the main speakers, and he mentioned my name to them because of my work with hospice. It was unexpected and a huge challenge for me, but I focused on sharing my story and revealing so much of my journey on a public stage for the first time in my life. It was received very well, and many people told me how important it was that I write my story. That certainly was the first time I ever considered doing that. This memoir is the result of that encouragement.

I have added that Reiki talk as an appendix to this book. In it, I describe bringing this spiritual practice of Reiki to both the AIDS patients and hospice patients I encountered and how my animal Reiki teacher, Kathleen Prasad, inspired me to bring this practice to animal shelters, which enriched my life. These human and animal encounters changed my life. I am so grateful for the opportunities I was given.

I want to share one special note of appreciation I received from the hospice team concerning my work with them, which touched me deeply:

> *I would like to acknowledge the outstanding work of Bill, our Reiki Practitioner. I have had the good fortune to witness two outstanding presentations done by Bill to increase our knowledge of the profession regarding the benefits of Reiki therapy. Bill exudes serenity and compassion. His gentle, unassuming manner draws others to him. Those who heard him speak were truly inspired by his words and his anecdotes regarding the power of Reiki to provide healing even when there is no cure. I am truly grateful to be able to work with Bill and even more grateful that our patients can benefit from his healing and compassionate touch.*

As my years with the VNA were coming to a close, there were some signs, which I did not detect at first, that my life, as I knew it, would change dramatically. When my youngest sister, Agnes, visited me in 2010 on her solo car trip across the country, I became aware of her declining health issues. She took sick on her return trip while in Pennsylvania and needed to fly back to California and have her car transported back to her home.

My older sister, Mary Ann, was dealing with serious health issues and collapsed one day where she was living with my nephew, Bobby, and was in a coma for an extended period before being snatched from death to begin a long healing process, but she was never able to return to her home and lived out her remaining days at a nursing home in Mamaroneck, NY. She died in April 2012 very peacefully with her eldest son, Bobby, at her side.

Shortly after Mary Anne's death, I had a serious car accident on my first day back to work with the VNA, after Mary Ann's burial in Newport, RI. I informed my family about the issue immediately, as I did not want to hide anything from them, and I knew they would support me through this without judgment, which they did.

Fred May, a chaplain at the VNA, whom I called from the scene of the accident, came over to drive me home. I was very shaken and traumatized. Later that morning, Susan Andrews, my co-worker, a nurse practitioner, Reiki practitioner, and friend, came over to see me and took me to the ER to be seen, as my wrist, by that time, had started to swell. The brothers never questioned me or did anything but support me. I was so grateful for that.

Later that month (May 2012), I visited my sister in California, as she had not felt well enough to travel back east to Mary Ann's funeral. Agnes' health was to be a major concern for all of us for the next two and a half years. There are periods of time in your life when things start happening so fast that you have no control over them, and all you can do is be present for them as best you can.

In October 2012, "Superstorm Sandy" struck New Jersey and Asbury Park. I remained in my apartment during the storm with my cat, "Sammie," whom I had gotten from the shelter two years earlier. As an aside, when I went to the shelter that day, I had my eyes on a brown and white kitten and told the adoption counselor I would be back the next day for it. When I came back, there had been a miscommunication. They gave me a seven-year-old cat named Sammie, who had been in the shelter for over two years, and they were thrilled someone was taking him. What could I do? So I took Sammie. And we made it through the storm together for the following three weeks without electricity.

Interestingly enough, during the storm, I decided to start my memoirs. So, as I had nothing else to do during the storm and its aftermath, I began to write. Now, ten years later, I am finally completing my story.

In June 2013, my great-niece Lauren and Dan were married at a beautiful wedding on the beach in South Jersey, and I was honored to do one of the readings. It was the most enjoyable family event I ever attended. I just made up my mind I was going to enjoy myself, and I did.

Also, during that month, I decided to retire from the VNA. Huge changes from the top down were happening in the organization, and it was just time. It was a great ten years and an enriching ministry. I had never worked so closely with such a hard-working and dedicated group. I just learned and grew so much in being present to people and their caregivers at the end of their lives.

Also, during my last year with hospice, I became aware of a teacher of Qigong, Maxine Gunther, in Lincoft, NJ, and attended some of her classes. At one point, her teacher from California, Dr. Roger Jahnke, taught a full-day class, and I was completely captivated by him and wanted to learn more. He told us of a class at Omega Institute in Rhinebeck, NY, near West Park, to be held in July 2013. I signed up for this class, and this started me on a journey that would end up in Santa Barbara, CA, in November 2015. After over 300 hours of training, I would become a certified Integral Qigong and Tai Chi teacher.

So, it became apparent that I would not go into a "do nothing" retirement mode. It was a change of pace for me, but I also seemed to need to continue pushing myself. I struggle to find a balance during my day, but it is not happening easily. I don't judge it; I live my life each day trying to be conscious when I need to step back and take some time. I realize there is probably an unhealthy work ethic present, which I don't seem to be able to let go of. And all very much connected to intimacy issues. But also, I am who I am, and that is okay.

One more thing. In November 2014, Darwin Chan, a graduate student from Columbia University, called me to interview me for a paper he was putting together as part of his studies. He had noticed the New York Reiki Conference online and picked up my name from there.

I had a two-hour interview at my apartment in Asbury Park, which was followed up with a couple of phone calls later when he was writing his paper. He kept returning to issues of my being a gay man and how that fit into being a brother and what my affiliation with the Church was on both the gay issue and practicing Reiki. I wrote him an e-mail with the hopes of bringing some clarification to these matters.

November 21, 2014

Hi Darwin,

You seemed interested in bringing up my issues with the Church—especially around homosexuality and Reiki, which is absolutely fine. Still, my one or two brief responses may not have been helpful.

Yes, I am a brother in the Roman Catholic Church, and I have strong feelings about the Church's positions on issues that strongly affect people's lives. This may seem contradictory, and I would like to clarify that.

I never had a strong identity as a person when I joined the brothers in 1951. I embraced the identity of brother, and that satisfied me for many years. It was difficult for me to ask to leave the comfortable role as a teacher and start the long journey of finding out who Bill Stevens was. Now, I am Bill Stevens, who is a member of the Congregation of Christian Brothers. Before, I was a Christian Brother, making that my complete identity. This is a very subtle distinction, but it made a profound difference for me.

In the '40s and '50s, when I grew up, there were no role models of a gay man in society, much less within the Brothers Community or the Church. I never knew there was such a classification. There were subtle or not-so-subtle hints that you were not manly by using terms like "sissy" that I grew uncomfortable with. I knew it was a negative term but did not think much about it.

In our training in the religious community, there was minimal, if any, discussion of sexuality. You were just expected to be celibate, period, if you wanted to stay. So it was not until well into my '40s, when in the 1970s, gay men began to reach the headlines of our newspapers, and I realized this was a term I could relate to. I pondered it for many years, and it wasn't until the '80s, during the peak of the AIDS crisis, that I began to interact with gay men, and I was able to acknowledge to myself that I was a gay man. Because of these men's courage, I could free myself and accept who I was. Then, I slowly came out to friends and family. I never felt a need to make any big public statement, nor do I feel that need today, but when and if it comes up in conversation or otherwise, I do not hesitate to share it.

No Church should shut people out. When the Church said gay men were intrinsically evil or objectively disordered, this bothered me. And I began to distance myself from the hierarchical church that felt this way about me. I do not believe anyone should attend church if it is not nurturing that person on their spiritual quest. When I was young, I was told if you were not Catholic, you would go to hell fire—this was their truth. I no longer believe that. We can find God within ourselves and do not need a mediator to do that. But if there is a group of people or a Church to whom we can relate and who nurtures us on that path, then that is a great gift to us.

A few bishops' statements on Reiki were disturbing to me because they influenced people to view a beautiful healing method as evil or wrong. I dismissed this and never altered anything I was doing, but I know it affected others, which saddened me.

Some people feel called to make noise about such actions by the Church. I do not feel called to do that. But I don't let it influence my life or choices. I think people are speaking by their feet. They are leaving in droves. But they are still gathering together in small groups and nurturing each other. I facilitate such a group.

I hope this is helpful. I just felt you were looking for more from me, and I was not satisfied with my minimal responses, which might have been misleading.

Looking back on it now, I was probably giving him much more than he needed or was looking for. But maybe it was just something I was doing for myself. I don't think I had written anything so clearly before on where I stood on the Church and my sexuality.

What does one do with one's life when one lets go of formal ministry?

24

Deeper Healings

*I would love to spend more
time with you
Words frozen on my lips
Fear and shame continue
To bring on my apocalypse.*

I continued to pursue deeper healing in my life. It was on and off because it was scary, and I ran away and came back. But I never abandoned the pursuit of it. When I was ready, a teacher always showed up. I don't know why I was always gifted with that, but I was. Hunter Flournoy is a teacher who has been there many times for me throughout my journey. I have done weekend retreats at Kirkridge in PA, made conference calls, and had one-to-one sessions with him. This is what Hunter said about his journey:

From the Earth traditions, I learned to respect and deepen my relationships with the living spirits of this world. In the Toltec tradition, I learned to free myself from judgment, fear, and doubt, and I learned to love myself for the first time in my life. In the Christian mystical tradition, I learned to love every being as the Divine Beloved, and from the Sufi tradition, I learned to surrender myself into the arms of that Beloved. Now, finally, I am an apprentice to Life itself, my own Life, our Life; it has become my guide, my friend, my lover, my child, and my greatest work of art.

It has been my greatest pleasure to support my own clients and apprentices in giving themselves extraordinary levels of freedom in their lives. The peace, fulfillment, success, and joy that blossoms in their lives move me so deeply in my own journey! I feel so grateful to all of my teachers, whether they were clients, healers, teachers, mystics, or keepers of ancient medicine traditions. Whatever the teachings, tools, and techniques they passed to me, the most important thing each of them offered was an invitation to the deepest awareness, the most unconditional loving, and the opportunity to express power and beauty in every thought, word, and deed. I have been holding out this same opportunity to my clients in many settings, including traditional psychotherapy, intuitive freedom coaching, Toltec breath work, workshops, healing sweat lodges, poetry, storytelling, and sacred journeys around the world.

I hesitated to share the poem below, which I had written after one of my retreats with Hunter. It gives you a little glimpse of how powerful they were for me. But to help you follow the poem, I wanted to share a little background. Tom was present at one of my first retreats with Hunter, and I was very much drawn to him. I struggled during that retreat not to make myself a bad person for this. Then, a year or two later, he walked into the conference room late at the beginning of the retreat—a very unexpected surprise. At one point, Hunter chose to have us form a circle and place a hand into the circle with our eyes blindfolded to grasp the hand of a person who would be our partner for the next exercise we would do together. I found myself holding Tom's hand. Then, the last stanzas refer to Tom entering the last gathering of the retreat in drag.

I've traveled roads to Kirkridge
Many times before
Why make another pilgrimage?
What am I looking for?

We gathered in the sacred room
Waiting for one more
As we settled on our cushions
Tom walked through the door.

My heart missed a beat
How can this be true?
I never thought we'd meet again
Such longings had turned blue.

We talked about our light
And things we do not see
The Divine shining bright
Through the shadows within me.

One on one with Hunter
Brought memories back to me
John was truly present
Looking out for me.

"I want to spend time with you"

Words frozen on my lips
Fear and shame continue
To bring on my apocalypse.

And then, we formed a circle
No, it will not be
But yes, there is a God
He placed his hand on me.

Look into your partner's eyes
Where your Beloved lives
Take in all the love
That such a lover gives.

Come into that wordless place
Where hearts become one
Enter into timeless space
Where two souls can embrace.

"I would love to spend more time with you"
Words frozen on my lips
Fear and shame continue
To bring on my apocalypse.

Morning sun arrived
And once again, bells chime
Back into our sacred place
To gather one more time.

Someone else was in the room
But how could that be true?
A woman had entered through the door
A beautiful one, too.

A burst of light went through my soul
And a truth was set free.

It had taken over 80 years
To realize this in me.

Tammi in the center
In all of her attire.
Sharing something deeper
Which only could inspire.

Tom was now ready
To return to his abode.
"I would love to spend more time with you"
Words frozen on my lips.

I'm sorry, forgive me
Is it not meant to be?
Deep thanks for creating
Such new life in me.

Bill April 2014

In 2009, I took a huge risk for me: attending a workshop for men. The description of this workshop, Body Electric, was advertised thus:

> This workshop teaches men how to connect with their deepest centers of pleasure by using exercises that involve breathing, stretching, and touching. Men had the chance to shed inhibitions that blocked access to their erotic selves. The setting is playful, safe, and honoring, allowing each man to focus on the entire body and gain full access to feelings and desires. Participants learn how to give and receive full body pleasure that heightens

body sensations and awakens deeper centers of
knowing. Just a few benefits are a greater acceptance of self as an erotic being; awareness of
spiritual dimensions; a rediscovery of the joy of
being alive.

It took me months to allay my fears about taking this
step. I often put it on the back burner and just worked,
worked, worked. And then, when I did slow down, I
knew something was missing in my life, and I did not
want to die without giving it attention.

Part of me just wanted to let things be and stay in my
comfort zone or take a risk, which would counter how I
lived my life. I wanted to let go of the guilt, fear, and
hatred of self. I wrote my brother, sister, and a couple of
friends and asked for their support in taking this step.

My friend Joan was amazingly supportive. She wrote
some beautiful, supportive statements that eased many
of my fears.

*Is it a betrayal of your vow? Your part of the bargain
was not something the Church should have ever asked
of you. When someone asks us to give away our humanity to belong—well, that is not a valid contract.*

*You cannot hide your sexuality—you have tried to
do this, but we who receive you feel your sexuality . . .
it is subtle because you have made it that way . . . but
it is seductive, sexy, and present whether you are
aware that it is expressed or not—it is present and received.*

*You entered a service requiring you to deny some-
thing profound about yourself—now you want to feel,*

use, and express it. These are steps you have been tak-
ing for a very long time. Now, you want to reach con-
gruency and peace, and no one else but you has to
know how you are congruent.

Both my sister and my brother were supportive. That
was so, so incredible.
My sister wrote:

> *You view yourself tougher than anyone else does and*
> *hope the workshop will be a step to set you free. . . . I*
> *am so proud of you. I love you so much, and I want to*
> *hear everything from the beginning to the end (that*
> *you want to share)—go with the flow of the moment*
> *and enjoy the "ride," so to speak. Scary is always an-*
> *other name for excitement. We are meant to grow up*
> *right up until the time we leave the earth, and for all*
> *we know, maybe we have an eternity of growing. So*
> *yes, you are on the right path. Have a ball!!!*

I wrote everyone who supported me this note after
the two-day weekend:

> *Of course, just taking that first step was the hardest.*
> *Without all your support, I would never have taken it.*
> *To give a detailed description of the weekend would do*
> *it dishonor and leave it wide open to misinterpreta-*
> *tion. Each session and practice had its purpose and*
> *built on what went before—to isolate any one event*
> *would be misleading. So I will not do that. All I can*
> *do is let you know what happened to me.*

I brought my history, which I shared with you, to the experience. I always felt I had to deny my sexuality both growing up and even more so in my religious life when I took a vow of celibacy. My body certainly knew I was a sexual being, but I always tried to hide that fact (as if I could).

How healing to be with a group of men who could celebrate their sexuality and not be ashamed or guilty. We had an incredible facilitator with a team of eight equally dedicated and gifted men who were there to assist us in taking those steps we were ready to take and to letting go of the fears and inhibitions we were prepared to let go of—that we had learned from family, church, and society.

Statements I can make today which come from the deepest part of my being and ring true for me are:

- *I am a sexual being—it is part of being human (everyone knew but me)*
- *Sexuality is only good.*
- *The Church is so, so, so, so wrong!* (This is me—church was never mentioned on the weekend.)
- *Healing happens; you can't make it happen; all you can do is be ready to receive the gift. I was ready and was healed from many wounds.*

I am fully aware that part of this may be the euphoria from the experience, but it seems deeper than that. It will just have to play itself out.

So, thanks again for your support. I feel a heavy burden has been lifted. A lot of sadness and anger has

gone. And a feeling of peace and excitement for the fu-
ture is there. I am not closing any doors and hope to
keep all possibilities open for myself.

I end with memorable notes from one very powerful
session:

I screamed, yelled, and sobbed for all the negative
messages given to me

Then came quiet and peace

I was wrapped in a cocoon and heard the words, "I
will always be with you."

The Universe created us as we are, a great crea-
tion.

Other remembrances from that session:

J appeared over me
So close—smiling/dancing/joy-filled
I cried,
Told him how much I missed him,
Cried for lost time—for a lifetime without sexual en-
joyment

Deep healing occurred.

I had one very negative retreat experience at one point in my life, at what I thought would be a healing retreat, which was not healing but very eye-opening. A couple of times, I attended a Dignity meeting in Greenwich Village in New York—a Catholic support group for gay men. I was uncomfortable most of the time, but I tried to give it a try. One of the leaders spoke of a retreat that would be held on the West Coast—close to where my sister lived in Malibu for gay priests and religious. So, I said to myself, why not? I signed up and made the long trip.

It was a lovely setting, but I still felt uncomfortable around so many priests. At the end of the day's agenda, they had a social in the evening. People just talked, and I listened, as usual. When I heard priests speak about going to bars, meeting people, and having relationships, it pushed me over the edge. I did not know what to do about it. I shut down completely. I should have just left and gone to be with my sister, but I stayed in my room the remaining days except for meals and conferences.

I have never experienced such shock and anger in my life. It was my stuff. I kept asking myself the question, why did I spend 50 years of my life going to confession, and not once was I told to stop confessing making a sexual thought bad? The reality hit me so very hard. To this day, my body reacts to this memory.

Each time I faced my fear of intimacy and sexuality and placed myself in the hands of a teacher at a retreat or workshop, I was deeply rewarded. It opened the door a little bit more, and I briefly caught glimpses of freedom, which I could not sustain once I left that safe space. But I healed many wounds and no longer made myself a bad person for having sexual thoughts. The shame and guilt gradually disappeared. The bottom line was I had fully absorbed all these messages, and no one lifted those messages from my heart despite my weekly confessions to those who could. And that was sad.

As I left the institutional church and turned towards meditation practices that I learned on Buddhist retreats and immersed myself deeply into my studies of Reiki and Tai Chi, I have been able to embrace a spiritual journey into the Mystery, which has no name, no dogma, and no belief system. And that is indeed a healing place. I built solid walls around myself when I was young as perceived protection, and slowly, brick by brick, I am taking them down and bringing myself closer to a freedom I have never enjoyed before.

John McNeil, whom I mentioned as one of my most cherished teachers, died at the age of 90. As a Jesuit priest, he condemned the writings of Cardinal Ratzinger, who ordered him to keep silent or be expelled. He continued speaking. His courage and honesty only endeared him to those he spoke for. He had made arrangements to be buried on the grounds of Kirkridge Retreat House in PA and requested on his tombstone to be written, "Here lies a gay priest who took a chance on God."

Don't let anyone colonize your mind.

Epilogue

A nyone who knows me would be surprised by this outburst of self-revelation. I also was surprised by my strong desire to do this. It has been both cathartic and healing for me.

I have rewritten this epilogue several times. As I said in my dedication, I wrote this memoir for myself. I wanted to thank and acknowledge the people who have touched my life in different ways. But it is only possible to mention some. You know who you are. I sincerely appreciate that our paths crossed, and I hope you gained as much as I did from the encounter. Of course, so many of you are no longer with us, and I will be joining you soon.

To my family, thank you for being there for me. Not all families do this, but you did it big time. I wanted to be as honest as possible in sharing my reactions and experiences during the different parts of my life. This was my life; through these encounters, I grew and evolved. I would not trade the experiences I have had with anyone else. They made me who I am today, and I am deeply grateful.

In July 2005, Parker Palmer wrote:

> Vocation is something I can't not do for reasons
> I'm unable to explain to anyone else and don't

fully understand myself but are nonetheless compelling. Our deep gladness meets the world's deep needs.

Self-care is never a selfish act—it is simply good stewardship of the only gift I have—the gift I was put on earth to offer to others.

Our true self is the self that wants nothing more or less than for us to be who we were created to be. To be whole means to reject none of your dark or light side but embrace all of it.

During the COVID pandemic, I moved from New Jersey back to New Rochelle, NY, where I joined the brothers over seventy years ago. I live with a small community of brothers off the Iona University campus. Zoom has come into our lives since the pandemic, and like for so many others, it has enriched my life. It has allowed me to remain in contact with the many groups that previously nurtured my life, and I have also been able to add many new groups since arriving here.

I teach an occasional Reiki class, publish a quarterly Reiki newsletter, and facilitate a monthly Reiki healing circle. I continue to teach my Tai Chi and Qigong classes and remain connected to two long-standing spiritual support groups—Mystics Anonymous and Something New. I am also presently in the middle of a Year to Live class with seven other people facilitated by Patricia Faye Marshall, preparing for our death. It has been such a positive and uplifting experience that has given me a new energy to live my life fully in each moment given to me.

Also, I am taking a Zoom class on the New Cosmolo-
gy on the Deep Time Network facilitated by Stephan
Martin. This class is opening my mind to the New
Universe story based on the writings of Thomas Berry
and Brian Swimme. It is very exciting and life-giving,
and expanding my horizons.

In 2009, I met Mary Ann Schoettly, RCWP, at a retreat house during lunch and had a delightful conversation with her. She told me that she was on the verge of
being ordained a Roman Catholic woman priest in
Pennsylvania and invited me to her ordination. I did
attend the joyous occasion but could not be part of the
community she formed in North Jersey because of the
distance. Mary Ann died in 2014, and Michael Corso, a
former priest who helped Mary Ann form this community, was chosen as their new facilitator. During the
pandemic, Zoom allowed me to become part of this
Sophia Inclusive Community, where everyone is welcome.

One of my longest mentors was Rev. Michael Dowd,
who recently died, which was an irreplaceable loss. Jim
Bender expressed it well when he wrote of Michael: "A
brave, bold, positive, humble, intelligent, good-hearted
man who made a unique contribution to humanity at
this unprecedented time." Michael was a pioneer in
warning us about the consequences of Climate Change
and the End Of The World As We Know It. I followed
his talks and videos on and off for over 20 years. He and
his wife traversed the United States in a trailer for
almost 30 years to bring his message to anyone who
would listen. Karen and Jordan Perry and those who

loved him dearly are determined to keep his vision alive. With his wife's permission, they have preserved and expanded his website (postdoom.com). Val Christensen and Peter Melton facilitate a weekly Thursday evening gathering called Collapse Acceptance Alliance, which evolved from Michael Dowd's work and is something I have made part of my life. It is a support group for people worldwide who are dealing with the reality of collapse all around them. Many use this group to move out of isolation, receive support, and share their fears and grief. Such frank exchanges help me to try to live my life in a positive, loving way as I attempt to reach out to the human and nonhuman community around me.

I want to close my memoir by leaving you with two teachings that have strengthened me. The five precepts created by Mikao Usui from Japan, who died in 1926 and was the Founder of the System of Reiki. And a simple mantra used by Bishop Spong, who died in 2021, almost a hundred years later.

The Five Precepts

Just for today:
Have the intention to let go of your anger or hatred towards another being.

Just for today:
Have the intention to let go of your fears and worries that you hang onto.

Just for today
Be grateful for everything.

Just for today
Be true to your way and your being
on this planet, Earth.

Just for today
Be compassionate to yourself,
and be compassionate to all beings.

Bishop Spong

- *Be fully alive*

- *Love wastefully*

- *Be all that you can be*

Really, what else is there?

Reiki at the End of Life:
New York Reiki
Conference

*When you truly serve, there
is no giver and no receiver.*

I want to share a little about myself and how Reiki came into my life. After teaching for 24 years in the Christian Brothers schools, I trained as a chaplain at the Hospital of St. Raphael in West Haven, CT. This type of training is called Clinical Pastoral Education. This 9-month in-residence program exposes you to patients in life-threatening situations while being supported by intense supervision and peer review.

I cannot adequately describe how that experience transformed my life and gave me tools that I have returned to again and again, even to this day. I entered religious life at seventeen and dedicated every moment to becoming this "ideal brother" who was held up for me to follow. It was a miracle that I found myself, at the age of 45, with the opportunity to discover who Bill was for the first time in my life.

I can clearly remember the first day on the hospital floor. You were sent on the floor to learn by experience.

That was the way it was. This was not book learning. I found a man who was actively dying in the first room I entered, in the pulmonary intensive care unit. I would not have chosen this room to start my training if I had known that. His spouse was with him, anxiously watching his final moments. I am not proud of what I did next, but I rationalized that I needed to move on to my other visits on the floor, and I left the room. I was completely unaware of my fear, my anxiety, and my unresolved issues around death. And so I moved on to another room. For the first and only time while I was in the program, a nurse found me and sent me back into the room after the patient died. And I got it; all the spouse needed was someone to be with her. It was not about me.

We wrote verbatims during the training. These are exact accounts of our visits—preferably the most troublesome ones. Then we sat with our supervisor and six peers, and we went over that visit moment by moment. A description of the environment, what the patient said, and how we responded—word for word. Here, we began to learn what was going on inside of us during the visit, most of which we were unconscious of, those things that drove our actions and responses. We did this five days a week for nine months. You can imagine the stuff that came up for each of us. We would never have had the courage or skills to look at those issues by ourselves.

After the first three months, it was suggested to me that I no longer wear my black suit and collar in the hospital. Wow, how terrifying that was for me. Nothing to hide behind anymore. I remember walking to the hospital in my red plaid jacket and tie the next day. No one batted an eye—they greeted me as if nothing had changed. But something changed in me—I never wore the black suit and collar again. I realized that when I walked into a room, all the person saw was the collar and everything they carried about that—good and bad. But they did not see me. When I visited with my collar, some people would throw me out as I appeared at the door. Now, I could walk a few steps into the room and let them know I was a chaplain before they threw me out.

One of the profound lessons I learned in the CPE experience was that Bill was enough. My role as chaplain was merely a ticket to enter the room. But then I had to learn to be quiet enough to listen to those places where I run and hide behind that role. I discovered I needed to continue to do my homework, to find those times when my fear, my pain, my anxiety, and my unfinished business were preventing me from really being present to where the patient was. It was an ongoing process.

Henry Nouwen wrote a book called *The Wounded Healer.* He said each of us is called to be a wounded healer, not because we have no pain but because of our pain. Recognizing and embracing our common human condition is not easy. But I learned that it is because of my woundedness that I can know, understand, and have compassion for another.

Compassion is defined as "permission to come alongside." This is a boating term, but how wonderfully it expresses being with someone at the end of life.

My CPE experience taught me that HUMAN PRES-
ENCE AND UNDIVIDED ATTENTION ARE THE
GREATEST GIFTS WE CAN OFFER.

My AIDS Experience

This experience was followed by ten years of chaplaincy
work in Syracuse, NY, and New Brunswick, NJ. It was
at St. Peter's Medical Center in New Brunswick that I
met my first AIDS patient in the mid-80's. At this time,
when a person entered the hospital with a diagnosis of
AIDS, it was a death sentence.

When I walked into the room of my first AIDS patient, I wanted to run out of the room—I had such fear
and a sense of powerlessness. Somehow, I fumbled
through that visit but certainly did not feel I was pastoral. It was similar to my first experience starting my
CPE program in the Pulmonary Intensive Care Unit. So
I sat with that experience with the AIDS patient for a
long time. To continue this ministry, I had to get help
for myself.

At the time, I sought help from the only outreach
organization in New Jersey—the Hyacinth Foundation.
An organization created by gay men to care for their
own and teach others about the disease. And so I
learned about AIDS and, in the process, went through
their Buddy training program as well and volunteered
to be a Buddy to someone with AIDS. His name was
Leonce Charbenaud—a gay man from Texas and a drug
user as well. I learned about his life and the pain of
losing ALL your friends to the disease. I learned about
enabling and being manipulated, and I learned about
the pain of addiction. This man was determined to

become clean before he died, to find a relationship, to become an actor, to come out publicly to make a difference, to fight the stigmatization, and to educate kids about the epidemic and how to be safe. He had quite an agenda for himself. He became the actor he always wanted to be and helped put on a play about AIDS and brought it to the schools in NYC. After the play, the actors would sit on the stage and talk with the kids about AIDS. He touched many lives and spent his remaining days just giving.

Because of people like this, I felt drawn to do more for the AIDS community. So I left the hospital and, over the next couple of years, created a non-profit organization called Chrysalis Ministry. This was modeled on an existing organization in Washington, DC called Damien Ministries, which was founded by a lawyer from Texas named Lou Tesconi, who sold his practice and joined the Carmelites, a religious order of priests, only to discover a few months later that he was HIV positive and found himself on the street not knowing what to do with his life. He created a residence for people like himself, on the street with AIDS and nowhere to go. He also created a retreat program, inviting people anywhere in the United States who had AIDS to come and spend four days together—all expenses paid.

I desired to offer services to the AIDS community that no one else was offering. I studied for a year to be a massage practitioner, and during that time, I heard of a chaplain in San Francisco offering Reiki to AIDS patients and caregivers at the hospital where he was working. I searched for and found a Reiki master in NJ and signed up for a Level I training.

I went to AIDS Coalitions in the State. I offered them the services of Chrysalis Ministry, which included pastoral visits to wherever the AIDS patient was, massage and Reiki sessions to those open to receive it, and four-day retreat programs. That is really where we got the name. We offered a Chrysalis—a safe space for anybody with AIDS—free of charge—a safe environment for those who were living stigmatized, isolated lives from family and friends whom they could not share their secrets with.

Based on Damien Ministries' model, these retreats were transformative for everyone who volunteered to help and for those who bravely attended. People came out of hiding: some were homeless, some were in AIDS residences, some were from shelters, some were teachers, some were clergy, and some were from Wall Street. They all had something in common, and they healed each other. We did this three times a year for ten years. We had 60 people on our four-day retreats and 30 on our couples retreats on weekends.

We invited different presenters over the years, always had small groups so people could share their stories and receive support, offered massage and Reiki to everyone, and always had a healing circle to remember those who had died—where people were able to share publicly for the first time the names of loved ones in this safe environment—the names of friends and family members who had passed. And we also had fun times—people in this environment could live their lives again without fear and shame.

Before I move on to something else, I would like to share one story that gives a glimpse of the power of these gatherings. I ran a support group in Perth Amboy, and at one point, I realized that one man, let's call him Bob, stopped coming to the support group because of the presence of gay men there. He was just very homophobic. I never pushed him, but I did tell him about the retreat program, as I knew he was getting sicker and may benefit from the experience. One day, he let me know he would like to attend. At the beginning of the retreat, we did a thing where each person drew a name, and that person was what we called your prayer partner. You had to keep that name secret during the retreat; you would pray for them and do little acts of kindness toward the person. All in secret. Also, you were asked to make a gift for them from the arts and crafts table, which would be given to the person at the last exercise of the retreat.

So, on the last day, we were in this large circle with 60 people, and each person would get up and say something about their prayer partner and give them a gift. Well, the biggest Queen in the group got up and walked towards Bob. He went up and stood in front of him and told him how much he had thought of him during the retreat and how much he loved him. He then took a necklace from around his neck and said how precious the necklace was to him. It had been given to him by his grandmother, and he wanted Bob to have it. He then placed it around his neck and gave him a big hug. Bob and all 60 of us were blown away. Extraordinary things always happened during those days.

I used to go to AIDS clinics in hospitals, and when the clients came in to see their doctor, they could, before or after their appointment, receive a massage or Reiki session. I also did this during support groups at different venues. A person could leave the session and step in for a half-hour treatment. At one of these sessions, I gave Reiki to a man who had mental health issues and was struggling with drug addiction as well. At the end of the session, he was in a very different state, not attributable to any substance he had taken. He told me he had had the most spiritual experience he ever experienced. He could not expand on that any further—but was visibly affected. Reiki did that—it brought people to a different place—a peaceful, quiet, deep place. Quite profound.

I was a Level I practitioner at this time, trying to do what I was taught. I rarely felt anything myself when offering Reiki, so I was touched by how Reiki truly gave the person what they most needed.

I used to visit AIDS patients in the hospital who were at the end of life. One particular person I remember was in pain when I was visiting, and I offered Reiki to him. After a few minutes, he told me that the pain had dissipated. I was as surprised as he was. It helped me realize that it is not about my experience but what the person is experiencing that counts. Later, whenever I walked into the room, he would say, "Here comes my pain medication." I often thought the nurses must have thought I was sneaking something into him.

I used to go to Bailey House in Greenwich Village, an AIDS residence housing some 20-30 people, and I spent the day there offering massage and Reiki. They were incredibly responsive to the sessions as the disease had made them "the untouchables"—their bodies covered with the purple blotches from the Kaposi sarcoma. Leonce, who was homeless for a while, was eventually able to live there, and from there, he got an apartment of his own. Leonce then found a relationship and moved to Washington, DC, where he died a couple of years later. I was able to facilitate his memorial service at Bailey House and publicly acknowledge the role he played in my life.

I had open heart surgery in 2001 and also closed Chrysalis Ministry. At times, I felt there was a connection between the incredible number of people who died during those 12 years and my heart failure. I remember once holding Leonce after he learned of the death of another friend as he sobbed in my arms for over twenty minutes. The loss of his friend was just a last straw which opened up his heart to grieve for the hundreds of those he had lost. Towards the end of this ministry, I found I was experiencing similar reactions. When someone I hardly knew died, I would find myself sobbing. And I then learned the depth of grief that multiple deaths can cause.

These years with Chrysalis were the most significant years of my life. I felt this was why I was on the planet Earth. One of my later teachers taught me that when you truly serve, there is no giver or receiver. I always felt this ministry to be a total gift.

Seeing people totally rejected by family, church, and friends, courageously living their own truth, and facing their own deaths at such an incredibly young age, with such dignity, are images that stay with me and are very humbling.

My VNA Experience

I took a sabbatical year, and during that year, I heard of an End of Life Training program in San Francisco run by Frank Ostaseski, the founder of a small Buddhist Hospice. He invited 25 healthcare professionals nation-wide to meet once a month for four days over 12 months—nurses, doctors, social workers, volunteers, and chaplains. He and other outstanding professionals in the field led a program to help us learn how to be totally present to the person and their family as they entered the dying process. I connected with the VNA Hospice in NJ to do fieldwork as I completed this program.

Upon graduation, I asked the VNA if I could be a part-time chaplain with them. After six months, I proposed to the Director that I offer Reiki to the clients along with my chaplaincy ministry. She had me meet with the Board of Directors to receive their approval. They approved a trial run to see how it was received.

I began by offering to teach Reiki to interested nurses or staff. About six people responded. I also offered a treatment to the Director, who put it off at first. I told her to call me when she was stressed out. It didn't take long. She called me, and we had a session after her stressful morning, and she became a believer.

I continued working as a chaplain and would offer Reiki whenever a nurse made a referral. This was slow at first, but then the nurses began to see it was making a difference with the clients and their caregivers and began to make more referrals to the extent that I was working more as a Reiki practitioner than a chaplain. Eventually, we hired a second practitioner and then a third because of the number of responsive clients.

Family members consistently asked me, "What is Reiki?" I always struggled to find an answer that would not turn off the questioner's interest in experiencing a Reiki session.

When I have thirty seconds on the phone to explain Reiki to an inquiring family of a hospice patient, I say, "Reiki is a spiritual healing energy practice that many people find comforting and relaxing." For some people, the words "spiritual," "healing," or "energy" are turn-ons, and for others, they are turn-offs. It seemed to help determine an interest in Reiki during a brief phone conversation.

My only equipment is a tablet with my music and a folding stool. When I enter the house, I assess where it is best to offer the session. The majority of the time, it is suitable just where the person is at the time. That is why I bring my stool, as it can usually fit right beside the person wherever they may be—sitting in a chair, lying on a couch, or lying on a bed. Where the person is most comfortable works for me—I am the one who needs to adjust. I want to share some of my earlier hospice experiences and one very recent one.

The Story of Jim

One day, a nurse called me to tell me a man with a lot of anxiety was at the end of his life and asked if I would come to give him a treatment. I had minimal conversation with him but took the time to tell him what I would do. It did not take long before he went into a deep Reiki slumber.

The next day, the nurse called to tell me that his wife had called to say he would like me to return. I once again offered Reiki to him, and he went into a deep Reiki slumber. The nurse called me the next day and told me that he had died twelve hours after the session, and before dying, he had reconciled with his son and had died peacefully, surrounded by lots of love from his family.

The Story of Sarah

Sarah, a Jewish woman in her 60s, was distraught over her diagnosis and had spoken to the social worker several times. The social worker felt she was stuck, and more words from her would not help. She called me to be with her—"looking for anything that would help." When I arrived, I sat beside Sarah on the couch; I told her I would like to play some music for her and would like to place my hands lightly on her body. Almost immediately as I began, she had an emotional release, crying out, "I have everything to live for—a beautiful family and wonderful grandchildren."

The social worker went in to see her later that day, said she was alert, verbal, and calm, and asked for some French fries. I saw her about seven times after that. Each time, she was more relaxed and seemingly more peaceful. In the later visits, she began to lay on the couch for the sessions and was always in a deep sleep when I left.

After she passed, her family told me that she had told them after my visits, she had always felt "like a new person." The family said they had referred to me as the Voodoo Doctor—but knew whatever I was doing was helping.

The Story of Jack

Jack was a construction worker and had a rough exterior. He was a Roman Catholic but had refused to see the chaplain. He had cancer of the esophagus and was a very quiet, reserved man. The nurse asked if I would come in to give him Reiki.

We had minimal conversation. I offered him Reiki as he lay on the couch. He did not seem to have any external reaction to the session. I returned for a second session the next week, and he was much more open to receiving it. And he went into a deep sleep shortly after I began.

The next day, the nurse called me and told me he was a changed man. He said he had never felt so good in his life. He was so happy I had given him the treatment. It took him to another place—a peaceful, calm place—and he felt so much better for it. The fear and anxiety he had exhibited earlier in the week were no longer there. He asked for a priest and received the last sacraments. I gave him one more treatment before he died a few days later. He had called his wife during the night.

She came out to be with him while he was lying on the couch. And when she went back to bed, he passed quietly.

My rational mind always seeks an explanation. But the bottom line seems to be over and over again that this very spiritual energy travels to where it is most needed on a physical, emotional, spiritual, or mental level for the person's highest good.

I do nothing. The person does nothing.

The Story of Joan

Joan, one of our nurses from the VNA, had bravely fought cancer for several years while continuing her work serving others. At the end of her life, she had a lot of anxiety and knew of Reiki but had never experienced it. She had reached a point where she was willing to try it, although she could not understand it or see any reason why it would be helpful.

The family asked me to come, and Joan was open to it. She found that it put her in another place—a very peaceful and relaxed place. She asked me to continue coming as often as I could.

One day, when I arrived, I realized that she was in the dying process. The family had surrounded her bed. I indicated I would do whatever they wished me to do. They said they would like me to do Reiki for her as it was something she had told them made such a difference for her.

The family left the room, although one or two usually stayed. I began offering her Reiki while a VNA nurse sat beside her. After a few minutes, she started taking her last breaths, and we called the family back into the room. They were with her as she breathed her last.

The Story of Mary

There was a time when I was asked to visit a home without much information about what was happening. When I entered the door, I went into a darkened room with people lining the walls in chairs and a large double bed in the middle of the room with a woman in distress lying on the bed with two of her children lying beside her, and she was moaning very loudly with each exhalation. Her husband was at her head as I opened my stool, sat at the end of her bed, went into my meditation, and offered her Reiki. After a half hour, her husband needed to go into the other room, and he offered me his space closer to her. I continued to offer her this energy. Forty-five minutes later, she became more peaceful, and her moaning subsided. She passed a couple of hours after I had left, and her husband told the social worker she had been struggling so much during the past three weeks, and he had not seen her in such peace as she was after the Reiki session.

The Story of David

Another time, the social worker asked me to come to the home of a man dying of cancer who was in great pain despite the pain medications he had been receiving. He was open to giving Reiki a try. Whenever I called for the next six weeks, he was always open to my coming. He told the social worker that from the very first treatment, he had never again had the pain that he was experiencing when we first met.

The Story of Margaret

Last month, I was called to the home of a 63-year-old woman who was close to the end of life and in discomfort and had asked for Reiki. When I arrived, she was surrounded by her large family of siblings and children. They stayed while I played soft music and opened my stool beside the bed. After the session, her daughter asked me if I would say a prayer. Not knowing her faith denomination, I shared a generic prayer and invited the family to share anything they wanted to say to Margaret. Each of them told her how much they loved her and how much she meant to them.

The next day I came, they told me how much she had rebounded after the session. And I continued to go for six more weeks. She was in various stages of discomfort when I would arrive but always went into a deep Reiki slumber during the session. I began to give sessions to her daughter and son, who were keeping long vigils and were near a point of total exhaustion.

One day, I got a call from her daughter, who asked me if I could come over that day as she had taken a turn. She was no longer conscious or communicative. The end was near. It was at that visit that they told me that she had frequently shared with them all the things that were happening to her during the Reiki sessions— seeing her deceased loved ones, wonderful landscapes, and different spirits. All quite beautiful to her. I gave her what was to be her last session. The family kept vigil all night, and then her son told them she was not going to let go unless they left the room. Her son told her they were going to bed, and they all left. Fifteen minutes later, her daughter went back into the room and found that she had passed. They did not call the VNA but surrounded the bed once again, and each family member was able to say whatever they needed to say. They called the VNA at 7 am and were so grateful that she had died at home, where they were able to do this.

I am at a loss for words about what these experiences are doing for me. Again, it is just a pure gift. One of my teachers once said how great it is that we get paid to go into a person's home and meditate for 45 minutes. How true that is.

My Animal Reiki Experience

Before I end, I would like to share my experience as an animal Reiki practitioner and teacher. About five years ago, I heard about an animal Reiki teacher, Kathleen Prasad, who lives near San Francisco. She is internationally recognized as a pioneer and leading animal Reiki educator. I took some of her teleconference courses, then decided to attend one of her classes at Bright Haven in Santa Rosa, CA, and spent a week there. Bright Haven is run by a couple who opened their ranch-style home and acres of land as a hospice and care for a variety of animals who are disabled, elderly, and at the end of life—horses, dogs, cats, hogs, goats, geese, swans—whatever comes to their doorstep— really dedicated people.

One of the things about Reiki that is so wonderful for animals is that you don't need physical contact or touch, and it is gentle and non-invasive. So when we talk about animals who are sick or have been traumatized or abused or have some issues that they need healing from, Reiki can address all of these issues—physical, mental, emotional, spiritual—whatever the issues are. Reiki can address them all from a gentle, non-invasive space.

I learned that Reiki is more of a meditation we do with animals rather than an active treatment as we might do with humans. It differs from other holistic modalities because of its passive and gentle nature.

This makes it ideal for traumatized animals, wild or captive animals, such as exotic animals in enclosures, deer, birds, squirrels, and those who visit us in our backyards, and, of course, for our pets or our friends' pets.

It is such a beautiful way to connect to other species and see them at a deeper level. When you connect in the Reiki space with another being, you know that we are all the same, connected, and one.

That brings us back to the spiritual ideal that the founder, Mikao Usui, had while working with his students. That is, going deeper within ourselves and uncovering our true nature, which is being one with all things.

My classes with Kathleen have been incredibly in-formative and challenging. I have never experienced a more dedicated and driven person to bring this gift of Reiki to animals. She is president of the Shelter Animal Reiki Association, whose mission is to promote the use of Reiki in animal shelters, sanctuaries, and rescue facilities worldwide through education and training. I encourage you to look at her website, which gives you information on all the SARA teachers volunteering to make this a reality with the locations of the shelters around the world where they work.

During a six-month internship with Kathleen, which I did from my home in New Jersey, I was able to engage in 50 Reiki sessions with animals in different settings— in a person's home or a distant session from my own home, at shelters, or foster homes.

I will share one experience I had:

The Story of Benz

One day, when I went into an SPCA shelter, I met a volunteer fostering a recently rescued dog named Benz, who came from one of the southern states. It was quite a challenge.

He had a lot of aggressive behavior towards the male gender, which made it difficult for him to be adopted. I worked together for several months with the volunteer in the shelter and at her home, where she brought him for brief periods.

When I first went outside his cage at the shelter, he was very aggressive. As I sat quietly in my meditation and offered Reiki, he would slowly back off and stretch out on his mat into a restful place.

When I first went to her home and sat in meditation to offer him Reiki, he would pace around the room and initially go up to the second floor to stretch out and relax. After a few sessions, he would go to a nearby couch and fall into deep Reiki slumbers during the sessions.

We were optimistic, but he continued to be quite aggressive towards her husband. After some scary incidents, he was brought back to the shelter, and it was determined he was not adoptable and needed to be put down.

I asked if I could give him some private Reiki sessions before this happened. The person in charge found a supply closet that would provide us privacy. She said she wanted to be with me and would bring some work with her while I was offering Reiki.

I offered Reiki to him the last two days before he was euthanized. They were two of the most powerful experiences I had had with him. He was just so receptive. At one point in the session, he approached me as I sat on my cushion stretched out in front of me and stayed there for an extended period in a deep Reiki slumber. It was the first time he had ever done that. The person in charge never did any work. She was just totally mesmerized by what was happening.

I was out of town when they put him down. But they did it very sensitively. They invited the volunteer to come and be with him and hold him while he was given a Big Mac, and they euthanized him. I later did a memorial service for the volunteer and offered her Reiki during that time.

I want to end our time together by leading you in one of Kathleen's meditations for offering Reiki to an animal for their healing. I invite you to participate and bring to mind an animal you would like to remember during the session.

Be comfortable with your spine nice and straight so that your energy can flow.

Have your hands on your lap with palms facing upwards. Close your eyes.

Set your intent that you are open to receive whatever you need most for healing at this very moment.

And with each inhale, feel the energy moving in through your nose, filling your body with energy all the way down to your hara (an energy center located two or three fingers below your navel, right about where the sacral chakra is).

As you breathe in this beautiful energy, you can image it as a healing light—flowing through your nose down into your body and down to the Hara.

As you breathe out, see this energy expanding outward through your skin, into your aura, into the room, and out into the universe,

So breathe again through your nose, filling your body with healing light down to the hara, and breathe out, expanding this light into the universe.

Breathing in, connecting to the hara, and breathing out, expanding your light into the universe.

So take a moment and continue this breath at your own pace, and with each breath, feel yourself relaxing more and more and feel your light getting brighter and brighter and more expanded with each breath.

Let your breath return to normal and sit in that beautiful space of energy you created with your breath—feeling yourself relaxed and expanded— bright and open.

Now, bring to mind an animal you would like to connect to energetically and offer healing to— whichever animal comes to mind right now is perfect.

See it with you right now—their fur, their color—see how they look. Now, look deeper and see their beautiful light, essence, and spirit.

And now, please invite them into the beautiful energy space around you. Invite them to step in and share healing with you for as much or as little energy as they are open to receiving; it is entirely up to them.

Just feel yourself holding this beautiful space of light. Your invitation is very open; it is entirely up to them. They are in charge, and we will sit and hold the space for whatever they need.

And as we sit and feel our connection—energetically, you may feel some sensation in your hands, tingling, heat—a sensation in your heart—an emotional connection—a feeling—it is the energy. You may feel something in your head or your mind. You are very relaxed, and you are going very deeply into a quiet space. This is the connection with the energy of the animal that you are feeling.

Just relaxing and connecting.

If your mind wanders, bring it back to the hara breath—breathing through your nose, connecting to the Hara, and expanding on the out-breath. Then, let go again and sit in that space with your animal.

And realize that you already have everything you need to assist your animal—all that wisdom, compassion, harmony, and peace—all that exists within you and will significantly help your animal.

And now, take a moment to thank your animal for being open to connecting and being your teacher in this journey of life and healing. Feel that gratitude from your heart for your animal.

Now, take a moment to set your intention to finish. Imagine you can bring all your energy back into your physical body and all your awareness back to your physical self.

You can put your hand over your heart and feel your groundedness and your center, and when you are ready, take a nice deep cleansing breath and slowly come back and open your eyes.

Kathleen suggests sitting with your animal for 30-60 minutes. Start with four sessions in a row on successive days because the sessions build on one another. Then, once or twice a week after that, and then once or twice a month. Every animal can benefit from Reiki for maintenance once or twice a month. It's like giving them a spa day.

She suggests 30-60 minutes because you will see an ebb and flow when we connect to them. They will relax, wake up, drink water, and then return and fall asleep. A dog may take 10 or 15 minutes to settle, but then it may finally settle, sleep for half an hour, and then wake up. We need to hold the space and let the animal walk into and out of the space. They take Reiki as an ebb and flow, not like a human being who may lie on the massage table for 60 minutes. Animals are more active and will take some Reiki and do something else, then return and take some more. One of the rules in offering Reiki to animals is that we let them be who they are and don't force them to lie on a massage table motionless for an hour; we sit and hold the space and let them move in and out of the space as they need.

This kind of session can be used for whatever comes up for the animal mentally, emotionally, physically, or spiritually.

These are just a few things I wanted to share to give you a taste of how Kathleen approaches offering Reiki to animals. On the sheet I have handed out, you will find her websites, where you can find all the information about her books, teleconferences, free monthly support groups, and incredible articles and stories from animal practitioners worldwide.

So, just learning all of this from Kathleen has been another incredible gift for me. I don't know why I have been so fortunate to have been exposed to such excellent teachers.

Thanks so much for listening. I enjoyed putting this together and want to express my appreciation and deep gratitude to Dave and Inoshi for their encouragement and support.

Appendix 2

My Family

Thank you mother. Please know your pain, your doubts, your disappointments and your incredible courage in the face of such hurdles, have paid off for all of us.

I put together different kinds of remembrances for the members of my family, in the order in which they passed. I wrote some, and some were written by my siblings. My family played a huge role in my life journey. I could not have gotten this far without each one of them. I wish we could have been closer, but the bottom line is we were there for each other when it counted, and what is more healing than that?

Dad (1986)

I am sorry, Dad, we could not have been closer. I regret not knowing you. I wish I had had the courage to change that. I know how much I missed you not being there for me in those times when I needed someone. And sometimes you were there, but I couldn't ask.

I now know why you were not able to be there physically at different points in my life, but that does not take away the pain that you weren't there. By the time I was in high school, and you were present, it seemed we were strangers. How much I wanted to please you and get your attention. I never felt I was someone you were proud of and wanted to be with. Or is that my stuff I am projecting onto you?

My deepest regret as a kid was never being able to see Joe DiMaggio at Yankee Stadium with you. It just never happened. Once, my mother said, you tried to get tickets. I was happy to hear that.

I do thank you for what you did for me, for all of us. I know it could not have been easy for you, and I have no idea of the sacrifices, pain, and struggle it was. I know you did not have ulcers, diverticulitis, kidney stones, heart attacks, and strokes because you didn't care. Your will to live and survive all of this so you could support our mother and us is a great example to me. You never gave up on life and, in your own quiet way, have deeply influenced my life. I think I am English all the way through—not a drop of Irish blood in me.

When I shared with my mother that I wanted to be a brother, she told me I had to tell you myself. I was now the third one to let you know. I don't remember much of that conversation, but I always remember you saying, "Always be yourself, Bill." And that I have tried to be faithful to. And it seemed to have

*caused a lot of pain for myself and others and maybe
even you.*

*I remember being on your back when I was young,
way out in the ocean in Newport at Easton Beach.
What a great feeling that was. I also remember playing ball as a family in Newport; I seemed to have such
fun then. Then you had to be away. I never knew why
as a kid, but you always came back. And I thank you
for that.*

*And lastly, Dad, you called me Bill. Thanks for
that. No one else in the whole family did. I never
heard you call me Bergin. That seemed to be something special between us. I only discovered very
late in life that I was named after your brother, Bill.
In 1980, I used that name as I began my new life.*

With love,
Bill

Alice (1990)

First, I want to share a letter Alice wrote to me on
12/22/57 while I was in Victoria, British Columbia:

Dear Bergin,
*By the time you get this, we may well be into 1958.
Boy, if I had the money, I would have been out to visit
you six times by now because I sure do have the time.
Being unemployed has one big advantage, and that is
I will get a fairly good income tax return this year. It*

seems strange that the government will owe me money because I didn't work for four months out of the year.

Another advantage of having extra time on my hands is to get to know New York City better. I've spent some wonderful hours in the New York Public Library, reading poetry, reading rare books, and looking at art collections. Until now, the library has been the building with the two big lions out in front of it. I was forever meeting people next to the lion on the right or the lion on the left, but I never got to go inside.

I've also been to museums and small art galleries from Greenwich Village to Columbus Circle. I have yet to take that famous nickel ride on the Staten Island ferry boat. You can ride back and forth all day for a nickel as long as you don't get off at either port. I also got to see a lot of foreign offbeat movies that would never come to New Rochelle.

Of course, I also look for work between these various wanderings, but no luck so far. To date, I still hold to the firm conviction that it makes no sense to work eight hours on a job that you feel is much less than what you are capable of. If something good does not turn up right after the new year, I'll get a part-time job typing for four hours a day so I will have enough money to keep myself from becoming dependent on family for spending money. To date, I have been living off my savings, but after Christmas buying, it will be completely shot.

Well, partner, I've reached the end of the road.
Have a nice Christmas or New Year or both.

Love,
Alice

In June 1990, my sister Agnes shared with me that Alice had cancer of the lung, which had spread to the brain, and there was no hope for her survival. I was in North Carolina then and would drive back that day.

Alice was the middle child, the third of five. After graduating from New Rochelle College, Alice was hired by Harper & Row in New York City as a production clerk and book designer, and she enjoyed every minute of her time there. She delivered galleys to editors and printers and did book design for the art director. Alice loved books and was very proud of her work there, doing what she loved. She had to leave that position as she experienced the first symptoms of schizophrenia, and she was never able to return to it. She dealt with this illness her whole life. In the '50s, there was not a lot they could do to treat this mental illness. Initially, she went to a private facility at St. Vincent's Hospital in Rye, New York. We did not speak publicly about it; it was like a secret. She underwent "shock treatments" several times, as it was the only treatment available that had any hope—such a frightening and terrifying image for both Alice and family—helplessness and sadness.

As years went by and money was not there to continue placing her in a private facility, when she needed help, she would go to the state facilities. She had continuous cycles. She went into the hospital and came out feeling better, went into a work program provided by the state, did well for a while, stopped taking her medication, and gradually went downhill until the next admission. And her life would play out around this cycle.

When you visited home, you never knew the Alice you would meet. She lived with my parents in their two-bedroom apartment all her life. At bad times, she would leave her bedroom, ranting and raving while walking around the apartment. My mother knew how to handle it. She would talk with her and help her to calm down. It would break your heart. At other times, she was the gentlest, kindest, most compassionate person you would ever want to be with, had a tremendous sense of humor, and was just fun to be around.

My parents supported her their whole life. They always hoped the next admission would be different. I don't know how they did it. There was no support for families at that time. And it was hush/hush in society. My parents were always there for her, even at the worst times. Sometimes, they would have to admit her because she was becoming a danger to herself and it was not possible for her to stay at home. Only those who have been there know the pain of leaving your child at an institution in those circumstances. But in later years, there were different medications, and you could see a change taking place in Alice. Her bad days were less frequent, and she could handle things much better. She even mentioned the "voices" in her head now and again.

When our nephew Paul married and had his first child, our grand-niece, Lauren, Alice was so excited, and it changed her life dramatically. She was incredible with her. She entered her world and played with her from the moment she entered the door until she had to leave. When she knew the date she would be visiting, she would go out and make sure there would be little gifts for her when she arrived. I know her greatest pain was not to be able to experience her second grand-niece, Hillary, who was born days before she died.

Agnes and my nephew Tommy flew in from California, and we spent time at the hospital supporting Alice after her diagnosis of cancer. My mother did make a trip to the hospital, but it was very difficult for her to maintain the visits. I was asked to speak with Alice about her wishes for continuing the chemotherapy. She clearly did not want to continue it, wanted everything that would keep her comfortable, and wanted to live as long as possible.

My sister Agnes and I spent that evening with her for a few hours. Just talking. It was such a sacred and blessed time. All three of us knew it was special. The conversation was easy. At one point, a Eucharistic minister came into the room and asked Alice if she would like to receive it. Alice said okay, but make it quick. She did not want any lengthy prayers. It was funny. But she was being herself.

Agnes stayed the night at the hospital in a room provided for family members. The following day, when she got up, she was told that Alice had passed away during the night. When the nurses went to her in the morning, she had already died. It was heartbreaking telling my mother.

My sister Agnes offered a beautiful tribute at the funeral mass and shared a powerful piece of writing she did days after the burial.

Alice

You taught us how to die.
Your poetry taught us how:
to live
to hope
to perceive
to dream
to laugh

You were surprised, Alice, weren't you . . .
You were overwhelmed by love . . .
Love from your family,
Love from your friends,
Love from strangers,
Love even deeper.

They came — word spread — days after you were gone:

> *"Alice opened my pill box each day."*
> *"Alice smiled at me each day."*
> *"Alice greeted me each day."*
> *"Alice did this kind of thing, again and again. . . ."*

For me? All these days, I haven't felt any guilt, Alice.
I'm surprised at that.

Yes, I did feel fear in my early years as a child and as an adult. Why? I feared for myself in a world of "craziness accepted as normal."

There lies the start of the strategy—none of us knew that an entirely different world existed beyond the four walls of our inner worlds: our antics, cellars, closets, and pain.

How could we? We were just infants.
How could we? We were just children.
How could we? We were deprived of teenage folly, fun, and rebellion.
How could we? We left, all but you, at age 17.

But when we knew you were ill, never to return, we returned.

Our resistance—the 100-foot-thick wall we sur-rounded ourselves with—broke down. Why the courage and strength to come back into terror, twisted confusion, mixed messages, a pit, a trap, a chain ready to pull down and swallow each of us up and grind us to the piece of shit (that we once perceived of ourselves)?

Why? We came for you.

Edward came out of hiding for one day.
Mary Anne made daily vigils until you said, "No machine."
Mother came with a cane, swollen ankles, and a pounding heart.

No—not this time—we barged right in
We held you up to the world.

We clothed you with the dignity you not only earned
   but had always.
We proclaimed your courage.
We shared your humor.

Most of all, each, in our own way, were on a mission
      To take over your heart.
      No more fear, just tenderness.

You said, "Leave," and we stayed.
Leave, we stayed and held your hand.
Leave; we stayed and listened to your fears.
Leave, we stayed and shared.

You accepted death, yes, but finally, Alice, you accepted
   our love.
I felt your love.

In childhood:
I feared for you
I feared for myself because I did not understand.

I heard you, night after night.
Cursing, mumbling, laughing, crying.
I pretended to sleep when wide awake.
I feared for you; I feared for me
Because I did not understand.

I was brought into your world, night after night.
I didn't speak up out of fear for you.
The depth of your inner world, the torment of your soul.
The secrets of your heart, the torment of your mind.

And oh, the pain that poured out.
I didn't tell, I didn't speak.
I feared for you; I feared for me.

Because I didn't understand.

I gave what I only knew how — loyalty through silence.
I kept your secrets. No one could ever pry them from
*   me — ever.*
I kept your pain, I kept your fears.
I kept your hurt; I kept your terror.
All locked up inside of me.

To be shared by no one so it wouldn't be ridiculed.
To be shared by no one so that it wouldn't be dirtied.
To be shared by no one so that it wouldn't be distorted.

I gave what I only knew how.
Belief in your hurt, belief in your anger.
Belief in your torment, night after night.
I yearned to wipe it away. I froze within.
I feared for you. I feared for myself.
Because I didn't understand.

I heard the blows; I felt the pain as though my own.
I heard the screams, piercing towards you.
My heart froze in empathy for you.

I felt the anger. I saw the anger.
I heard the anger thrown at you.

I fought back at them, for you
But only in my mind.

I screamed at them for you,
But only in my mind.

I told them off again and again
But only in my mind.

I feared for you; I feared for me
Because I did not understand.

I think you knew how loyal I was.
I think you knew how I was on your side.
I think you know how deeply I cared.

Why do I think you knew?
Through your silence, too,
I felt your love, Alice.
I only pray you felt mine.

Your little sister,
Agnes

Alice was the recipient of the Who's Who Poetry Honors for Outstanding Achievement in Poetry for 1990, presented by World Poetry Magazine in Sacramento, California, and received many other awards throughout her career as a poet.

One of the last poems she was writing when she died was dedicated to Lauren, her grand-niece, and was written on a yellow pad:

My Little Girl

She's pink as roses
and made of clay
when I see her
it makes my day
tiny hands and little
feet — whose steps will
some day stray away
from me to God

knows who — as if
I will accept it right
away.

But now that she is
such a Babe
I'll have my way
with her. She knows
it too and tries
to make me fall
in love with her.
She smiles and shouts
and waves her fists
thinks it's all great
fun.

Mother (1996)

What haven't I already said? Thank you for everything you did for me while I was growing up. I think we moved thirteen times before I graduated from high school; I don't know how you managed that. No matter what was going on, we always had a great Christmas. You would have all the stockings hung, and we could look at them at breakfast and then, of course, all the presents afterward. You always tried to get each of us the one thing we wanted most. Each summer, no matter where we were, we piled into the car and went to Newport, RI—sometimes during the whole summer or at least to Aunt Amelia's farm in Tiverton. You once told us how you would drive all five of us from Binghamton, NY, to Newport, RI, without a valid driver's license. You always did what you had to do.

You always made things work. How often did we go for a picnic in a state park or special sights in upstate New York when we were in Binghamton? And, of course, we always drove to Poughkeepsie, NY to visit Edward during his many years of training.

When we moved to New Rochelle, you tried to get me into Blessed Sacrament a month after school began. Brother Chapman told you there was no room, but you convinced him to take me. And look what happened.

You turned to the God you knew to help you through all your difficult moments. Without that, you absolutely would not have survived. You trusted and prayed and made sacrifices (like daily mass during Lent, daily rosary, or novenas), and your prayers were heard. But you did that for us, mother. Thank you.

I know it broke your heart when Alice got sick and had to leave the job she loved in New York. You tried to do everything you could for her. So little was known about schizophrenia in those days, and the treatments were quite terrifying. There was no assistance whatsoever for family members to quell your fears or give you hope. You stood by her all her life during tough times and periods of remission. It swallowed up your life.

How sad it was for you to see Mary Anne's marriage fall apart. You stepped right in without missing a beat and took the four boys into your house on Coligni Ave. You told me once you were determined that it would be a happy time for them as you remembered when it happened to you in the early days of your marriage when you went to Mama's with the five of us. You told me those days on Coligni Ave with them were some of the happiest days of your life and Alice's, too.

When I came back from the West Indies and became involved with family affairs, I almost drowned in them. I tried to please you, fix things, make things better, take some of your pain away, and feel responsible for things turning out how you wanted them to. I don't know why I took that on, but I couldn't let go of it. You never knew I went to years of therapy to change that, but I was never really able to let it completely go. I want to let it go now. I did my best, Mother. I never felt it was enough, but I tried my best.

I know you had a lot of good moments, Mother. You found it hard just to let us be who we were when it did not live up to what you wanted for us. You didn't have the luxury, like I did, to go to therapy and get help. I know you wouldn't hear of that. But very few people would have taken on all you did for 94 years. You can leave this world knowing that you had five children who went through their struggles but achieved much of what they desired in life. You had four incredible grandchildren who love and support each other and are living happy lives today (more than once, they have said it was because of your selfless generosity and love for them) and two fantastic great-grandchildren who are well on their way to extraordinary lives. And two incredible great-great-grandchildren who are emerging into their new lives.

Thank you, Mother. Please know that your pain, doubts, disappointments, and incredible courage in the face of such hurdles have paid off for all of us.

Mary Ann (2012)

Our family gathered in Newport, RI, for the burial of Mary Ann, my oldest sister and the mother of our four nephews. She died peacefully on April 22, 2012, while my oldest nephew, Bobby, was sitting beside her. Bobby alerted the staff at the nursing home, and they took all the measures they could to intervene, as she had requested. Then, Bobby let us all know.

My nephew, Paul, sent me an e-mail shortly after:

> *Sunday, April 22*
> *I just got home from a charity event in Philadelphia, and I spoke to Ed, Tom, and Bobby, and they told me what happened. As you saw from the last visit, she took a turn for the worse, and over the past couple of months, she had been sleeping more and more. I am so glad she went peacefully and was so afraid she would be placed on a respirator for months/years.*
>
> *It is very sad, but I truly feel she was ready. I luckily talked to her last night and told her about Lauren (how she had got engaged!) and Mary Ann was so happy about it.*

I responded to Paul:

This brings tears to my eyes, Paul. You have been a
wonderful son to her. What a beautiful parting gift
you gave her Friday night. Yes, we could not have
asked for a more peaceful death—having Bobby at her
side and talking with her when she passed.

Something happened within me those days following her death. I took it upon myself to arrange for her final service at the gravesite. I did not want something that was not real for those gathering together to say good-bye. I suggested not having a church service or a rented priest to say the final prayers at the cemetery, as it would not be something meaningful for most of those attending. We did not have a wake but gathered in Newport a few days later.

To friends or family members, we made it known that:

A private service will be held for the family at noon
this Thursday, April 26th, at St. Columba Cemetery,
465 Brown's Lane, Middletown, RI 02842 (401) 847-
4571. In lieu of flowers, donations can be made to
"The Northeast Wing Staff of Sarah Neuman at 845
Palmer Ave., Mamaroneck, NY 10543, in memory of
Mary Ann Stevens."

I came up to Newport the night before and, in the morning, went out early to the cemetery, before anyone else, to prepare. No one was in the small chapel on the cemetery grounds, and I was curious if anyone else would be using it before us. We were not told this, and I presumed we would be the only service that morning. I looked everywhere for chairs, found some, and set them up in a single row facing each other, with room for the casket in the middle. I placed a rose along with the program on each chair. When I left the chapel, I was alone and just gazed at the beautiful ocean view a few miles away.

And then I just had a profound experience. It was like I had grown up. I had owned who I was. I was making decisions because I thought this was the right thing to do. A few hundred yards away were buried my mother and her mother and father, my dad, my mother's brother and wife, and Alice. All had a substantial impact on my life in so many ways. Now I could do what I felt was right and not worry about what others thought; if there was any disapproval, it didn't matter. It is hard to put this in words—all I can say is that it made me very vulnerable and gave me deep joy as tears rolled down my face. Why had this taken so long to accomplish?

Then family members came, and yes, another party was coming for a burial and wanted to use the chapel. I wanted to give us as much time as we needed, so we pushed everything I set up against the walls, and when the other party was finished, we rearranged it.

Everyone was milling about greeting and supporting each other. It was so good to see that. Then we gathered in the chapel. I asked Edward to offer a closing prayer, Pheme to do one of the readings, Paul, to give the eulogy, Tom to read a reflection from Agnes, and I read part of a letter from Nancy, Sally's sister, who was deeply touched by the life of Mary Ann. Then some people in their seated places shared their thoughts spontaneously. And we played some reflective music in between.

Paul's thoughts:

> *If my mom were alive today, this is where she would want to be, with all of us. It hit me just a few years ago what it must have been like for her to wake up one morning as a single mom with four boys, no car, no real money to speak of, and just some limited secretarial skills. I don't know how she did it and how she handled the stress that would have gone along with that. But as kids, we didn't fully realize what was happening and what she was going through; we just went with the flow. And, of course, Ma and Pa were so supportive throughout and helped my mom and us all get through it.*
>
> *We may not have grown up in the most conventional of homes, and we didn't have much, but one of the things my mom always instilled in us was good values. She loved and cared so much for us. Although when she was rebounding from her collapse five years ago, there was a period when she said some funny things to Eddie and me, such as "Your face looks fat," we would laugh.*
>
> *But seriously, she always, and I mean always, supported everything we did—from Eddie playing drums, Bobby on the guitar, me staying out late with my friends and following Sally to New Jersey, and supporting Tommy moving to New York and California—she was never critical. We never had to worry as kids as to what Mom might think because she trusted*

us, supported and loved us, and wanted us to do anything we wanted, as long as it made us happy. Because of this trust, we all could have done bad things as kids. But we didn't. My mom instilled excellent values in all of us; she taught us to care about people and taught us right from wrong. And she taught us about family. We have always had a very tight family.

My brothers and I are always in touch with each other and make plans to see each other, and we always made plans about seeing Mom, especially Bobby, who saw her every day. We were also close to Ma and Pa and our uncles and Aunts—Edward, Bergin, Alice, and Agnes. From Ma, who we loved immensely and who loved my mom and her boys so much and how she helped take care of us all, and Pa, who sat quietly in his chair every day (except around 5 pm when he would have his watered-down vodka tonic and became a little feisty), Edward teaching us chess, Bergin picking us up on Thanksgiving Day and taking us by the New Rochelle High School where Iona Prep ruined the statue every year, to Alice and the love she had for Lauren when she was a baby and to Agnes taking us to our new home in Stanwood, where I met Sally and her wonderful family.

Some might say my mom may have been too relaxed on the rules with us, as we had the rock and roll band in our basement in Stanwood, and how people walking by our house would see Hobo, Puppy, and Little Olive Oil jump out the front window to greet them. We can only imagine what people were saying when the Molloys rolled into town in the quiet little neighborhood of Stanwood. But I am certainly glad we moved there, or I would never have met Sally and her family, and we would not have Lauren or Hillary here today.

Growing up, my mom had a very tough road and lived in many places. She would tell us many stories about those days, stories about how she walked two miles in a skirt every day in those cold winters in Binghamton with her knees getting numb, stories about living with Mama in Newport, and stories about the times spent in Tiverton. My mom was the family historian; she always remembered everyone and everywhere she had been, and that was a lot of places.

To name a few other memories. My mom taught us some funny expressions that you don't hear anymore, but expressions I will still say from time to time. causing Lauren and Hillary to ask, "What does that mean?" My mom used to say "Hells Bells" when she was mad, or when we went to bed, she always said, "Sleep tight, and don't let the jin jins bite." She also used to sing songs while we were growing up, like "Dance with the dolly with a hole in her stocking, her knees keep knocking, and her toes keep rocking," "Step right in, step right out, Daddy let your hair hang down," and "Big Bad John."

Last night, I told Sally a story about how my mom swam out beyond the waves at Jones Beach one day to get a ball of ours that had floated away. I remember being so impressed by how well she could swim and how brave she was to go out there with all the sharks!!!!

My mom had many legal secretary jobs over the years and was always carrying her steno machine around, and we always had boxes of steno paper in the house.

She finally learned to drive in the 70's and loved riding around town in her red Mustang.

My mom had a funny thing about my birthday. She always got confused. I used to celebrate it on April 22nd, then on April 19th, and then finally, one day, I was cleaning out her closet when I was about 17, and I saw my birth certificate and my birthday was April 18th. I loved calling her on my birthday, and after a few minutes, I would say, "Do you remember what today is?" And she would say, "Oh Paul, it's your birthday." Just like she did last week.

She also had a funny thing about her name. Was it Maryanne, with an "E" at the end, or Mary Anne, two separate words? I came upon her birth certificate a few years ago, and I have the answer. It is Mary Ann—two words, no E. My mom was also funny about socks. She never liked wearing them and must have had the toughest feet. And as Sally remembered last night, she always liked tucking her feet under herself when sitting on the couch.

I also remember how excited she was when we had Lauren. When I came downstairs in the hospital after Lauren was born, there she was, in the waiting room, with Bobby. My mom used to love it when I brought Lauren and Hillary to Ma's. We would play with balloons and bubbles and go on the swings in the back.

It was a miracle how she recovered from her collapse five years ago, and we really can thank Bobby for that, as he absolutely knew she would recover, and he stayed by her side until she woke from her coma. She lived a second life at that point, allowing us to get to know her better and in a different way.

When she started rebounding, I used to call her all the time and loved talking about the past and talking to her about our dad and the good times we had when we were young, like our frequent trips to Jones Beach and Saul's for hamburgers after church. I also loved talking to her about what it was like for her growing up during the Depression and living in all those places she lived. Over the past five years, we could frequently get her out for the day and take her to Harbor Island, the Larchmont Diner, and our old house in Tuckahoe.

Although my mom had a very tough life, she rarely complained. All my mom wanted to talk about was us. I would always tell her about Sally and the kids, and I bored her with endless work stories that she really seemed to care about. She loved hearing about Eddie and Sue and Eddie's music and his writing. She loved telling me about Bobby, his modeling, and the classes he was taking and loved hearing from Tommy about all his adventures in California with Alan. She loved telling me about Eddie's visits and Tommy's phone calls. And whenever I called, the first thing she would say was, "When are you coming again?"

She also loved it when we got her Presto and for the last few years loved getting pictures from Lauren and Hillary and seeing their boyfriends and their travels to Europe and the beach. She hung these pictures in her room.

It was nice on the night before she died. I spoke to her and told her about Lauren and how she got engaged. I was so excited when Lauren told me, and the first person I called was my mother because I knew she would be so excited, and she was.

So, how do you sum up such an extraordinary life that she led? I would say thank you, Mom, from all of us who are here today. We love you, we will miss you, and thank you for everything that you have done over the years for all of us and for all the love you showed us. You will be remembered always and will be in our hearts forever. And Mom, you will be happy to know that the Jin Jins never bit us.

Agnes was unable to travel because of her health issues but deeply wanted to be with us. On her cross-country trip, when she arrived back East, she made it a point to spend several afternoons visiting Mary Ann, who was at that time in a hospital in White Plains. She told me later that they were the most significant visits of her life and was so appreciative that she had been blessed with these times with her sister. She sent these words with Tommy to be read at the service:

Mary Ann,

This is my promise to you years ago. When you asked that on this day, I say some words for and about you, of course, I said yes and that I would speak from my heart to you.

Mary Ann, I feel that for most of my life, I have observed you from the outside. As a small girl, I was in awe of you; I put you on a pedestal and was always thrilled when you played with me. Over the years, I saw that wherever you went, people loved you. You were so beautiful and kind. To this day, the women at Maryknoll have never forgotten you and have great affection for you.

Much of your life was filled with conflict, trauma, and concern, which you met to the best of your ability and spirit. To me, if I had to pick a one-word description that I always sensed when you were around, it would be "yearning" — as expressed by George Eliot's quote:

> *It seems to me we can never give up longing and wishing while we are still alive. There are certain things we feel to be beautiful and good, and we must hunger for them.*

Life passes quickly, and I do not know if your yearning was completed — but I do know the great gift you gave to our family and the world; you gave us Bobby, Eddie, Paul, and Tommy, and from them came Lauren, Hillary, Sally, Sue, Alan, and Dan — now that is a lot of love you created. They have enriched my life from afar and near and always with me.

In recent years, I have witnessed the love between them and for you — how great is that! Personally, I will always cherish that one week I had with you at White Plains Hospital. Thank you for those days.

Some of my favorite words are in Revelation, almost written for you, Mary Anne, in celebrating your life and passing:

> *And God shall wipe away all tears from their eyes, and there shall be no more death. Neither sorrow nor crying, neither shall there be any more pain: for the former things are passed away.*

I love you,
Agnes

Later in the day, someone mentioned a really cute story that revealed so much about Mary Ann. One day, when Eddie was growing up, he came upon a bully who was picking on Tommy and Paul outside their house. Eddie had never been in a fight and certainly never encountered this situation before. The bully hit him in the face when he confronted him. Then Eddie heard a voice from the porch of his house saying, "Get him, Eddie! Get him!!" It was Mary Ann. Eddie not only hit him but messed him up. It wasn't easy being a single parent of four boys.

Agnes (2015)

AGNES STEVENS 1935-2015

Agnes Stevens, Founder of School on Wheels, died in Ventura, CA, after a long illness. Agnes was born in Boston, MA, on June 13, 1935, the youngest of five children. Two sisters preceded her in death. Surviving are two brothers, four nephews, two great-nieces, and four surviving stepchildren.

Agnes taught in Chinatown in both New York and Chicago, as well as "Little Tokyo" in Los Angeles while a Maryknoll Sister for 18 years. She later taught for 22 years in the Pico Rivera Public School System in the primary grades.

After early retirement, Agnes came across a book by Jonathan Kozol called *Rachel and Her Children: Homeless Families in America*, which influenced her to become involved with kids who were homeless. She worked part-time at a school in Venice, greeting and testing the educational level of kids coming from a homeless shelter. These experiences opened her eyes and heart, and she began formulating plans on a way to reach out to kids without a home. In 1993, she single-handedly founded School on Wheels, a non-profit organization still thriving twenty-two years later. This past year, over 3,000 homeless students were tutored by over 1800 volunteers. They also provided backpacks, school supplies, uniforms, bus tokens, and computers to over 6,000 homeless kids and received donations of 1.5 million dollars.

Agnes received many awards and recognitions over the years. Her twenty-year fight on behalf of homeless children was recognized in 2008 when Agnes was one of three women who received the World's Children's

Prize for the Rights of the Child, known as the Children's "Nobel Prize." Winners were chosen by a global vote from a pool of 17 million children in 100 countries. It is the world's most prestigious prize for defenders of children.

We took our time and did not rush anything. We made plans for a memorial service at Paradise Cove's Community Center on March 2nd in the late afternoon for about 100 guests. Everything was made available to us, along with free catering at the end of the service. People could not do enough. They loved Agnes.

At her memorial service, I said:

> *I am Bill the brother of Agnes, and I would like to both welcome you, and thank you for taking the time to be with us.*
>
> *I want to share with you a talk that Agnes put together in the early 90's on the occasion of her first speaking venture for the Toast Masters Club in Malibu. Her talk was entitled "A Call to Freedom," and it began this way:*
>
>> Everyone rest your eyes as I paint a picture: a rainy night, a young girl, 16 years of age, sitting on a window sill overlooking the wet streets of New York.
>>
>> In front of this window sill are bars. No, not exactly prison bars, but bars of a cloistered convent in the heart of the city.
>>
>> This girl was the only one awake at 1 am except for her friend, a cigarette. The occasion was the monthly retreat for students of a Catholic girl's high school.

As I sat there on the window sill, I knew I would remember this scene forever. Why? As I looked on the city that night I made a wish that "I want to experience everything in life."

I was the youngest of five children my father was of English and Scottish descent and my mother was Irish.

Due to my father's work, our years as children involved many moves throughout New England and other states, living in one-room places, in regular homes, and even in a "mansion."

Yet our experience as children was far from varied: isolation, control, the strictest of restrictions, were the rules we lived by.

We responded as children with our imaginations, our books, and our dreams.

My inner call for freedom was strong. At 19, I took my first step toward that freedom and I entered the convent. Yes, the convent was the haven of this freedom for me.

The training and discipline were tougher than the marines. But a new world opened for me because the community I joined was Maryknoll, whose work was worldwide.

I learned and experienced much, but I did not belong there. After 18 years, I took another step and left the convent.

How really free I felt at age 34 in a one-room apartment, not knowing the ways of everyday survival such as how to open a bank account but survive and learn, I did.

This new way of life, living and rubbing elbows with everyone opened my eyes to the injustices of society.

For the next two years, I took on an almost obsessive way of life, fighting for the rights of everyone.

I taught school during the day, but in all my other moments I took part in every march, every picket line, and attended every meeting for every cause that ever existed.

And then the matters of the heart took over. Again, I had no experience in this area—ever, and I fell head over heels in love with a widower with five children.

My freedom was curbed a little during those 13 years of marriage, but my mind was ever active. After the children had grown, the pain of divorce followed.

So I took my next step to freedom at age 50; I started my life over again as a single person. With a kitchen table on the top of my car and my personal belongings within, I left for Beverly Hills for a one-room apartment.

Yes, matters of the heart came up again and I experienced a few glorious but fatal relationships

This meant: time for an inner freedom journey, time to take that long hard look. In therapy, an inner shaking up had to be done. I did it and graduated.

Four years later, I took a walk on Malibu beach and saw some mobile homes. One week later, I was in escrow.

The peace and beauty of Malibu was well worth the agony of escrow and a monthly mortgage.

But growth cannot stop. I took early retirement from my school district for the freedom of being my own boss in my own business of tutoring.

In the day I work on a project in a school that serves homeless children who come from shelters, cars, or motels. And at night, I tutor students in Malibu and surrounding cities.

As a teacher, I am at my peak, a dream come true to bring all my experience to every child.

My mission is to children, to help them find the inner and only true freedom: of peace within; of choices; of hard work that pays off; of believing in yourself.

That is the road I am on now.

I know the doing part of my life very well.

So now I need to learn how to BE. And someday, my doing and being will intermingle as one.

Then, the wish of that young lady sitting on a window sill will have come a little closer to becoming a reality.

I hope that you, too, will always believe that your slightest or deepest desire can come true as you risk and travel the journey to your own personal freedom, whatever it might be.

And in all the highs and lows and in-betweens, my journey has been quite enriching and a lot of fun too. May yours be too.

(Agnes did not end her journey there—it had just begun. At age 58, she created a non-profit organization, School on Wheels, to reach out to homeless kids, inviting tutors from all walks of life to go wherever homeless kids were. She won numerous awards before her death. In 2023, SOW celebrated its 30th anniversary, having touched the lives of over 50,000 children.)

P.S.,

Agnes was my best supportive friend and my partner in crime growing up; I was often called a sissy in my younger years, while Agnes took on any boy in the schoolyard. She never gave up on life.

Bill

Edward was not able to travel to attend the service in Malibu but had sent some thoughts for me to share:

Agnes was the youngest of five siblings. I am the oldest. My baby sister, whom I have known for 79 years, has died. Where to begin?

Agnes had the gift of changing the lives of everyone she touched. And she made her way through the many pathways on which her life led her. I began to ask myself—Who is this amazing woman—what is her secret?

The first thing every day, she made her way to the beach, walking through the water's edge, thinking about the world, and her place in it and how the world works as she did her planning.

We are holding today's Memorial at the shore. Agnes's place of peace, her church, just as the homeless children were her congregation.

I think of the Tao Te Ching: Here is where she observes the world. She watches how things come and go, but trusts her inner vision. Her heart is as open as the sky.

Mostly on the phone, Agnes and I had long discussions about her philosophy of life. Her view was resolutely positive and optimistic.

Dr. Wayne Dyer inspired her confidence that impossible dreams are really possible.

But she was realistic, too. Yes, the universe is a friendly place, but the universe is also a good teacher.

She would say over and over again, "If a decision fails, it was not meant to be—I'm fine with that." She was an idealistic pragmatist. Does that make sense?

"With her heart open to the sky," she could care less about taking personal credit or blame.

Ronald Reagan, who was not Agnes's favorite president, famously said: "You can accomplish much if you don't care who gets the credit." Agnes and Ronald Reagan agree on this one point! Agnes wasted no time defending her ego. Her service to others was unstinting. Every bit of talent, insight, and energy she was blessed with, she spent on others. In the end, she had nothing left on the table to give. Buddhists call such people "enlightened." The Catholic Church calls them "saints."

At my parish last week, Agnes's passing was commemorated at a memorial mass. If you are familiar with Catholic mass, you will know that the congregation joins in prayer with others around the world and with all those, including saints, who have gone before us, and typically, at mass, some of these saints are addressed by name.

At this particular mass, the priest added "St. Agnes" to the list of saints. I was startled. I first thought we were talking about my sister. Of course, the reference was to Agnes, a Christian martyr who died in 304 AD.

In conclusion, I miss my sister terribly. I keep wanting to phone her, but her phone is disconnected. So I pray to her instead. I thank Bergin for reading this for me. Know that I am present here today with you, dear friends, whom Agnes loved so much, in heart, spirit, and prayer.

Tommy asked his neighbors and good friends Danusia and Cory if they could take us out in their boat to spread Agnes' ashes. There were some rain storms predicted for the whole weekend. We got a tentative go for Sunday, March 1, the day before the memorial service. Tommy, Alan, myself, Paul, and Catherine joined Danusia and Captain Cory at the dock and decided to go for it.

It was just another extraordinary moment. We could visually see rain storms over the water and along the shore a short distance away, and yet the skies opened up in front of us. We would be heading towards Anacapa Island, which was part of the Channel Islands. Tommy had chosen to spread her ashes in the cove by Anacapa, which, on a clear day, he could see from his porch outside his bedroom in Malibu. At first, we were told that the waters and winds were usually strong there and that we might not be able to get as close as we wanted. But when we got to the cove, the waters and the winds were calm, and we were able to drop anchor a mile offshore. It was just an incredibly beautiful setting, and it lifted our hearts as we left, knowing Agnes would rest in such a peaceful place. As we were driving home, we met rain. The following day, storms were predicted, but we had nothing but sunshine during the memorial service.

I had informed Sr. Grace Corde, a very close friend at Maryknoll, of Agnes's death and highlighted some of the dying process, and she wrote back:

> *The spaciousness and depth of my heart have grown a hundredfold, dear Bill. Your envelope arrived this*

morning—a sacrament of living love. You have opened to me the realm of light and love that is the spirit of your sister and my companion. Every word you have shared, from your own experience of Agnes, resonates completely with what I hold within me. There are no words to express how completely your sharing has activated the essence of my own knowing. Agnes entered my soul decades ago, immediately and directly. I knew her from a place within me that was a homeless child. We connected in this place of wound-edness without any need to express the totality of this gift in words. Somehow, we both knew that our only way to live was through a greater Love, a God, that is not recognized in categories or standards. Someday, I will share with you how she accompanied me into the very home that made me homeless. She did this without fanfare. She just gave all she had, and it was enough. Yes, someday I will share.

Dear Bill, I am so profoundly grateful that you embrace the spirit, the journey, the totality of Agnes' destiny. You have blessed her beyond imagining, and she is embracing you with all her heart. I cannot write too much now, for my spirit is so full, but how utterly grateful I am for you and to you. Now I am going to absorb all that you have shared—a blessing that will last forever.

With deepest gratitude, dear Bill,
Grace

On 11/8/06, Agnes wrote me an e-mail:

I came across this quote this a.m., and I like it.
> *"Life is not a journey to the grave with the intention of arriving safely in a pretty and well-preserved body, but rather to skid broadside, thoroughly used up, totally worn out, and loudly proclaiming — Wow, What a ride!"*
>
> *Agnes*

Yes, it was.

Edward (2016)

I wrote this after my brother's death:

Edward, My Brother

My mother was the last one in her generation — the last one standing. No one left to share the memories with. No one to ask — do you remember when?

I felt that sentiment very strongly these last few weeks.

Our big brother is no longer here.

The one who always had the right words would always listen and would never put you down. He would call you unexpectedly just to check on how you were doing and would have incredible wisdom.

And when a crisis arose, he would be so supportive in both the smallest and big things in your life.

He was a true brother to my three sisters and me. He was there when it counted, and if not by his physical presence, he would find ways to make you know he cared.

The oldest sibling receives a lot of attention upon their arrival into the world. But they also assume a lot of responsibility, by default, as other siblings arrive. And when you add the challenges of the Depression years and World War II, it can be quite awesome.

Our parents married in 1927, Edward was born in 1928, and four other siblings arrived by 1935. At that point, our lives changed dramatically, and Edward was old enough to be fully aware of just how our lives were impacted.

Once, Edward wrote:

> I have memories of Pa going door to door trying to sell Ma's jewelry so he could pay the electric bill. But the lights were turned off anyway, and we sat in darkness when the sun went down.
>
> Boiled potatoes with molasses dinners.
>
> Ma burst into tears when I asked her for a dime to bring to the Catholic school so the nuns could buy supplies for us. This fee was called "paper money". She opened her purse to extricate a few coins and flung the dime at me.
>
> The police banged on our front door at 7 AM, evicting us for non-payment of rent. Pa found two rooms downtown at the cheap, low-life Windermere Hotel, into which we were herded. Hookers cursing and screaming, running up and down the corridors. Ma pushed furniture against the front door of the room to barricade us from the unknown terrors outside.
>
> But things went better when World War II started – yes, everything was rationed. But Pa had an income. He would prepare "treats' for us. One of his best was a

*slice of white Wonder Bread, spread with fake butter
and sprinkled with granulated sugar.*

My brother set a high standard, which none of us
could quite live up to, but he never made us feel we
had failed in any way.

We were very proud when he entered the Jesuit order, and for many years, we made trips to St. Andrew
on the Hudson in Poughkeepsie, NY, to visit him.
These trips became part and parcel of our lives. My
father, a non-Catholic at the time, was brought to
tears listening to the hundreds of novices and scholas-
tics chanting their prayers in the huge chapel while
we listened from the balcony where the families could
gather.

Many years later, while at Canisius College in
Buffalo, NY, Ed listened to the deepest part of his being and had the courage to take the painful and courageous step to move in another direction. Such life
choices are not easy and can easily be ignored to one's
own detriment.

Ed first met Pheme Perkins, who had recently received her doctorate from Harvard University and
was teaching at Canisius College, when she challenged one of his statements during one of his lectures
which she attended.

They were to marry in 1977, and Ed got to know
her incredible extended family and found a deep happiness and purpose in his life. They moved to Boston,
and Ed found a position at Regis College, where he
spent many happy years, and Pheme continued her
teaching career at Boston College.

*And then, a day after his 40th wedding anniver-
sary, going out for his usual morning power walk and
using the sidewalk on the street on which he was
walking, on Sunday, June 11, at about 8 am, he was
hit and literally run over by a car backing out of the
driveway.*

*He was helicoptered to a medical center 30 miles
away, where he spent days in the ICU. He was of
clear mind and spoke with great difficulty but with
clarity, and was able to let the hospital staff know he
was grateful for their attention but wanted to enter a
residence hospice for comfort care, as any surgery
would be high risk with no guarantees. Pheme was
fully supportive of all his wishes and fought to have
them carried out.*

*He then spent 17 days at the Miriam Boyd Parlin
Hospice, where he received excellent care. He died
peacefully with Pheme and myself at his bedside on
Sunday, July 9, at 12:15 pm at the age of 88.*

*I was able to spend periods of time with him both
in ICU and hospice. On one occasion, I asked him
what he thought about death. He responded, "I am
curious." Another time, I asked him to be sure to let
me know what death was all about, and after asking
me to repeat the question, he responded, "Be alert."*

*I wasn't close to my brother growing up. There
was a five-year difference in our ages, which is a big
gap when you are young. We both went into religious
life, and we were geographically separated.*

*Our paths might cross at a Thanksgiving or
Christmas gathering with our family if we were both*

in the area at the time. It was maybe in the mid-nineties when Edward got Agnes and me to purchase a computer and begin to share info amongst ourselves about what was happening in our lives. This correspondence between the three of us was to continue for the next almost thirty years, and it changed our relationship with each other in many ways.

When my parents passed, and my sisters died one by one, we became closer and kept in touch by phone calls or e-mails more frequently. A couple of times we spent time together in Newport on a weekend.

After the burial in Newton, MA, I drove back to New Jersey, and a couple of days later, I went to the animal shelter with other Reiki volunteers to offer Reiki to the dogs. A couple of hours later, as I went to my car, I stopped and talked to a friend before driving home. As we stood by my car and talked, my friend mentioned that a butterfly was sitting on top of the baseball cap I was wearing.

We continued to chat, and my friend again mentioned the butterfly sitting on my head. She then went to get her camera to take a picture of this unusual sight.

There was a noise in the parking lot, and the butterfly flew away. We ended our conversation, and I got into my car. I then noticed the butterfly landing right above the door on the driver's side of my car and staying there. I got out of my car gingerly and just watched it. It eventually flew away, came back, landed on top of one of the windshield wipers, and nested there for a while, and I took a picture of it. It wasn't a

*beautiful monarch butterfly but really a dingy-looking
brown.*

"Be Alert"

*I live on the 23rd floor in Asbury Tower, facing the
ocean. One day in late August, I looked out my window shortly after sunrise and saw a dragonfly on the
screen—one does not see dragonflies at that height,
and I had never seen one in that area before. It was an
incredibly beautiful sight. It had no intention of leaving. Just stayed there. I had to leave first because of an
appointment.*

"Be Alert"

*When I shared this with Pheme, she mentioned that
when she was teaching that week, a dragonfly had
landed on her whiteboard in class.*

"Be Alert"

Thank you, Edward.

After the death of my sister Agnes, Edward wrote a
note to me which included these words:

> *It's becoming increasingly clear to me that the tru-
> est way to understand human life is not to overly
> stress HERE and then HERE-AFTER.*
>
> *Agnes and Mary Ann and Alice and Mother and
> dad and Mama and you and I are, all of us, essentially
> living HERE and NOW.*

Everything from the past and especially everything now make you and I and each other the unique entities that we each are.

Love is what binds each of us and everything in creation together.

To the extent that we understand this and make decisions based on this; we literally are living in heaven on earth.

Theologians have a fancy name for this called "realized eschatology," i.e., the so-called "last things" are best seen as "first things" and "here and now things."

So, Bergin, we're living in heaven with Agnes. Love pulls aside the veil that obscures this realization.

So now, we are living in heaven with Edward.

Printed in the USA
CPSIA information can be obtained
at www.ICGtesting.com
CBHW070739230724
11902CB00070B/556